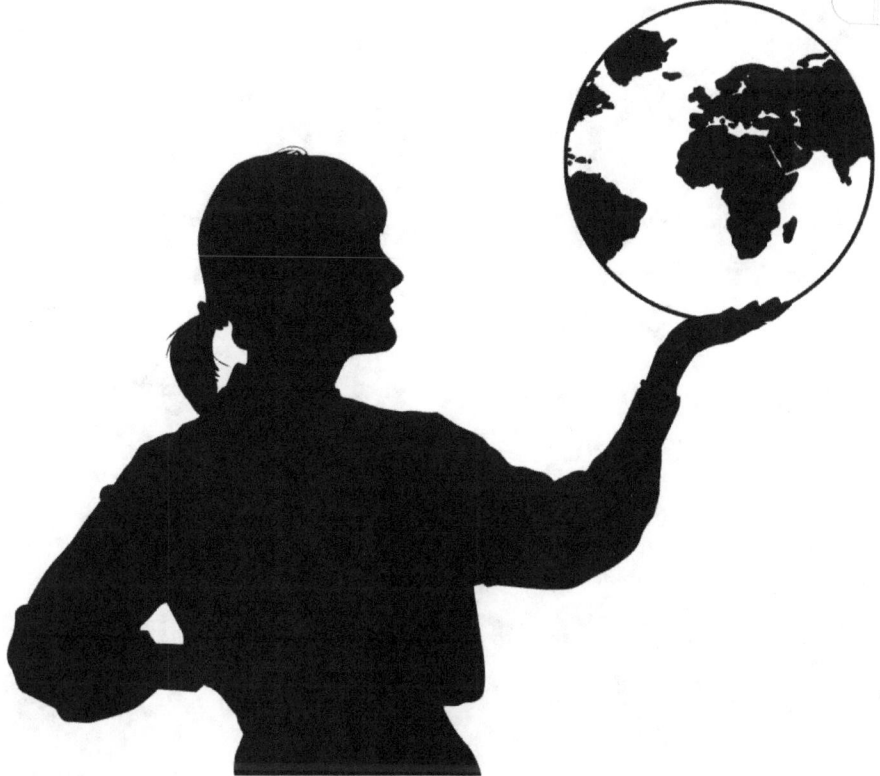

This Location Scouting workbook belongs to:

_____

_____

If you find it, please call:

_____

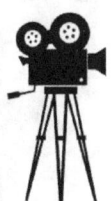

Just check it, to be sure everything is covered

First Printing: 2019
Mami6te
Bulgaria, Sofia
1680

Project:

Director:

Producer:

Location scout:

Scene: Scene Number:

Location name:

Address:

STORY

☐ **Storytelling:** Does the location meet the scene requirements and fit the director's tone?

☐ **Anachronism:** Does the setting fit the time period and story setting?

Notes:

SIGHT

◯ interior   ◯ exterior

YES	NO	**Indoor staging:** Does the crew, cast and gear fit inside?
YES	NO	**VFX Need:** Would anything need to be removed or added in post?
YES	NO	**Indoor staging:** Any special production design needs?
YES	NO	**Sunlight:** Any sunlight consideration?

◯ morning   ◯ noon   ◯ afternoon   ◯ evening   ◯ night

YES	NO	**Wide Shot test:** Wide frame acceptable?
YES	NO	**Wide Shot test:** Any problematicvisual elements in the frame?
YES	NO	**360 test:** Are there any problematic directions that should be avoided?
YES	NO	**Commercial clearance:** Any properties that require commercial clearance?

Notes:

SOUND

YES	NO	**HVAC:** Can you turn off the heating, ventilation and air conditioning unit?
YES	NO	**Reverberation:** Can you record clean dialog?
YES	NO	**Refrigerators:** Can you turn off any noisy ? appliances or refrigerators?
YES	NO	**Reverberation:** Do you need to dampen echoes in the space?

Notes:

SURROUNDINGS

- [YES] [NO] **Roads & Traffic:** Noise or continuity issues from vehicles or pedestrians?
- [YES] [NO] **Schools:** Noise or other issues connected with students?
- [YES] [NO] **Playgrounds:** Will noise affected the sound or will people be in the frame?
- [YES] [NO] **Factories:** Any noise generated from the machines or any road issues?
- [YES] [NO] **Gas station:** Any noise or traffic issues?
- [YES] [NO] **Parking:** Is there sufficient parking for talent, crew, and production vehicles?

- [YES] [NO] **Airports:** Noise or activity and traffic issues and concerns?
- [YES] [NO] **Air traffic:** Any significant air traffic overhead and sound concerns?
- [YES] [NO] **Subway:** Will subway noise fit to the scene? Will it affect sound recording?
- [YES] [NO] **Subway:** Will subway noise fit to the scene? Will it affect sound recording?
- [YES] [NO] **Train station:** Will train noise fit in the scene? Any train appear in the frame?
- [YES] [NO] **Staging Talent:** Is there a quiet place dedicated for talent, extras, crew?
- [YES] [NO] **Restrooms:** Is there a enough restrooms for all?

Notes:

WEATHER

- [YES] [NO] **Temperature:** Is there temperature control?

- [YES] [NO] **Rain / snow:** Will precipitation have a potential impact on the shoot?
- [YES] [NO] **Indoor:** Will sound from precipitation have a potential impact on the shoot?

Notes:

POWER

[ ] How many accessible outlets?

- [YES] [NO] **Access:** Does the electrical crew has access to the circuit breaker box?
- [YES] [NO] **Hair and makeup:** Is there a dedicated space and breaker for Hair & Makeup?

FACILITIES

[ ] How many people on set to every available bathroom?

- [YES] [NO] Access to **Water Shut Off** in case of emergency
- [YES] [NO] Access to **Gas Shut Off** in case of emergency

Notes:

CONTRACTS

[YES] [NO] **Contract:** Has the location owner sign the contract/location release?

[YES] [NO] **Insurance:** Does the production insurance cover the location?

Dates needed: Total number of days: Total cost:

Contact person:

Phone: email:

LOCATION SCOUTING CHECKLIST

Project:

Director:

Producer:

Location scout:

Scene: Scene Number:

Location name:

Address:

STORY

☐ **Storytelling:** Does the location meet the scene requirements and fit the director's tone?

☐ **Anachronism:** Does the setting fit the time period and story setting?

Notes:

SIGHT

○ interior   ○ exterior

YES	NO	**Wide Shot test:** Wide frame acceptable?
YES	NO	**Wide Shot test:** Any problematicvisual elements in the frame?
YES	NO	**360 test:** Are there any problematic directions that should be avoided?
YES	NO	**Commercial clearance:** Any properties that require commercial clearance?

YES	NO	**Indoor staging:** Does the crew, cast and gear fit inside?
YES	NO	**VFX Need:** Would anything need to be removed or added in post?
YES	NO	**Indoor staging:** Any special production design needs?
YES	NO	**Sunlight:** Any sunlight consideration?

○ morning   ○ noon   ○ afternoon   ○ evening   ○ night

Notes:

SOUND

| YES | NO | **HVAC:** Can you turn off the heating, ventilation and air conditioning unit? |
| YES | NO | **Refrigerators:** Can you turn off any noisy ? appliances or refrigerators? |

| YES | NO | **Reverberation:** Can you record clean dialog? |
| YES | NO | **Reverberation:** Do you need to dampen echoes in the space? |

Notes:

SURROUNDINGS

[YES] [NO] **Roads & Traffic:** Noise or continuity issues from vehicles or pedestrians?

[YES] [NO] **Schools:** Noise or other issues connected with students?

[YES] [NO] **Playgrounds:** Will noise affected the sound or will people be in the frame?

[YES] [NO] **Factories:** Any noise generated from the machines or any road issues?

[YES] [NO] **Gas station:** Any noise or traffic issues?

[YES] [NO] **Parking:** Is there sufficient parking for talent, crew, and production vehicles?

[YES] [NO] **Airports:** Noise or activity and traffic issues and concerns?

[YES] [NO] **Air traffic:** Any significant air traffic overhead and sound concerns?

[YES] [NO] **Subway:** Will subway noise fit to the scene? Will it affect sound recording?

[YES] [NO] **Subway:** Will subway noise fit to the scene? Will it affect sound recording?

[YES] [NO] **Train station:** Will train noise fit in the scene? Any train appear in the frame?

[YES] [NO] **Staging Talent:** Is there a quiet place dedicated for talent, extras, crew?

[YES] [NO] **Restrooms:** Is there a enough restrooms for all?

Notes:

WEATHER

[YES] [NO] **Temperature:** Is there temperature control?

[YES] [NO] **Rain / snow:** Will precipitation have a potential impact on the shoot?

[YES] [NO] **Indoor:** Will sound from precipitation have a potential impact on the shoot?

Notes:

POWER

[ ] How many accessible outlets?

[YES] [NO] **Access:** Does the electrical crew has access to the circuit breaker box?

[YES] [NO] **Hair and makeup:** Is there a dedicated space and breaker for Hair & Makeup?

FACILITIES

[ ] How many people on set to every available bathroom?

[YES] [NO] Access to **Water Shut Off** in case of emergency

[YES] [NO] Access to **Gas Shut Off** in case of emergency

Notes:

CONTRACTS

[YES] [NO] **Contract:** Has the location owner sign the contract/location release?

[YES] [NO] **Insurance:** Does the production insurance cover the location?

Dates needed: _____   Total number of days: _____   Total cost: _____

Contact person: _____

Phone: _____   email: _____

LOCATION SCOUTING CHECKLIST

Project:

Director:

Producer:

Location scout:

Scene: Scene Number:

Location name:

Address:

STORY

☐ **Storytelling:** Does the location meet the scene requirements and fit the director's tone?

☐ **Anachronism:** Does the setting fit the time period and story setting?

Notes:

SIGHT

○ interior   ○ exterior

[YES] [NO] **Wide Shot test:** Wide frame acceptable?

[YES] [NO] **Wide Shot test:** Any problematicvisual elements in the frame?

[YES] [NO] **360 test:** Are there any problematic directions that should be avoided?

[YES] [NO] **Commercial clearance:** Any properties that require commercial clearance?

[YES] [NO] **Indoor staging:** Does the crew, cast and gear fit inside?

[YES] [NO] **VFX Need:** Would anything need to be removed or added in post?

[YES] [NO] **Indoor staging:** Any special production design needs?

[YES] [NO] **Sunlight:** Any sunlight consideration?

○ morning ○ noon ○ afternoon ○ evening ○ night

Notes:

SOUND

[YES] [NO] **HVAC:** Can you turn off the heating, ventilation and air conditioning unit?

[YES] [NO] **Refrigerators:** Can you turn off any noisy ? appliances or refrigerators?

[YES] [NO] **Reverberation:** Can you record clean dialog?

[YES] [NO] **Reverberation:** Do you need to dampen echoes in the space?

Notes:

SURROUNDINGS

[YES] [NO] **Roads & Traffic:** Noise or continuity issues from vehicles or pedestrians?

[YES] [NO] **Schools:** Noise or other issues connected with students?

[YES] [NO] **Playgrounds:** Will noise affected the sound or will people be in the frame?

[YES] [NO] **Factories:** Any noise generated from the machines or any road issues?

[YES] [NO] **Gas station:** Any noise or traffic issues?

[YES] [NO] **Parking:** Is there sufficient parking for talent, crew, and production vehicles?

[YES] [NO] **Airports:** Noise or activity and traffic issues and concerns?

[YES] [NO] **Air traffic:** Any significant air traffic overhead and sound concerns?

[YES] [NO] **Subway:** Will subway noise fit to the scene? Will it affect sound recording?

[YES] [NO] **Subway:** Will subway noise fit to the scene? Will it affect sound recording?

[YES] [NO] **Train station:** Will train noise fit in the scene? Any train appear in the frame?

[YES] [NO] **Staging Talent:** Is there a quiet place dedicated for talent, extras, crew?

[YES] [NO] **Restrooms:** Is there a enough restrooms for all?

Notes:

WEATHER

[YES] [NO] **Temperature:** Is there temperature control?

[YES] [NO] **Rain / snow:** Will precipitation have a potential impact on the shoot?

[YES] [NO] **Indoor:** Will sound from precipitation have a potential impact on the shoot?

Notes:

POWER

[ ] How many accessible outlets?

[YES] [NO] **Access:** Does the electrical crew has access to the circuit breaker box?

[YES] [NO] **Hair and makeup:** Is there a dedicated space and breaker for Hair & Makeup?

FACILITIES

[ ] How many people on set to every available bathroom?

[YES] [NO] Access to **Water Shut Off** in case of emergency

[YES] [NO] Access to **Gas Shut Off** in case of emergency

Notes:

CONTRACTS

[YES] [NO] **Contract:** Has the location owner sign the contract/location release?

[YES] [NO] **Insurance:** Does the production insurance cover the location?

Dates needed: _____   Total number of days: _____   Total cost: _____

Contact person: _____

Phone: _____   email: _____

LOCATION SCOUTING CHECKLIST

Project:

Director:

Producer:

Location scout:

Scene: Scene Number:

Location name:

Address:

STORY

☐ **Storytelling:** Does the location meet the scene requirements and fit the director's tone?

☐ **Anachronism:** Does the setting fit the time period and story setting?

Notes:

SIGHT

◯ interior   ◯ exterior

[YES] [NO] **Wide Shot test:** Wide frame acceptable?

[YES] [NO] **Wide Shot test:** Any problematicvisual elements in the frame?

[YES] [NO] **360 test:** Are there any problematic directions that should be avoided?

[YES] [NO] **Commercial clearance:** Any properties that require commercial clearance?

[YES] [NO] **Indoor staging:** Does the crew, cast and gear fit inside?

[YES] [NO] **VFX Need:** Would anything need to be removed or added in post?

[YES] [NO] **Indoor staging:** Any special production design needs?

[YES] [NO] **Sunlight:** Any sunlight consideration?

◯ morning   ◯ noon   ◯ afternoon   ◯ evening   ◯ night

Notes:

SOUND

[YES] [NO] **HVAC:** Can you turn off the heating, ventilation and air conditioning unit?

[YES] [NO] **Refrigerators:** Can you turn off any noisy ? appliances or refrigerators?

[YES] [NO] **Reverberation:** Can you record clean dialog?

[YES] [NO] **Reverberation:** Do you need to dampen echoes in the space?

Notes:

SURROUNDINGS

- [ ] YES [ ] NO **Roads & Traffic:** Noise or continuity issues from vehicles or pedestrians?
- [ ] YES [ ] NO **Schools:** Noise or other issues connected with students?
- [ ] YES [ ] NO **Playgrounds:** Will noise affected the sound or will people be in the frame?
- [ ] YES [ ] NO **Factories:** Any noise generated from the machines or any road issues?
- [ ] YES [ ] NO **Gas station:** Any noise or traffic issues?
- [ ] YES [ ] NO **Parking:** Is there sufficient parking for talent, crew, and production vehicles?

- [ ] YES [ ] NO **Airports:** Noise or activity and traffic issues and concerns?
- [ ] YES [ ] NO **Air traffic:** Any significant air traffic overhead and sound concerns?
- [ ] YES [ ] NO **Subway:** Will subway noise fit to the scene? Will it affect sound recording?
- [ ] YES [ ] NO **Subway:** Will subway noise fit to the scene? Will it affect sound recording?
- [ ] YES [ ] NO **Train station:** Will train noise fit in the scene? Any train appear in the frame?
- [ ] YES [ ] NO **Staging Talent:** Is there a quiet place dedicated for talent, extras, crew?
- [ ] YES [ ] NO **Restrooms:** Is there a enough restrooms for all?

Notes:

WEATHER

- [ ] YES [ ] NO **Temperature:** Is there temperature control?

- [ ] YES [ ] NO **Rain / snow:** Will precipitation have a potential impact on the shoot?
- [ ] YES [ ] NO **Indoor:** Will sound from precipitation have a potential impact on the shoot?

Notes:

POWER

[ ] How many accessible outlets?

- [ ] YES [ ] NO **Access:** Does the electrical crew has access to the circuit breaker box?
- [ ] YES [ ] NO **Hair and makeup:** Is there a dedicated space and breaker for Hair & Makeup?

FACILITIES

[ ] How many people on set to every available bathroom?

- [ ] YES [ ] NO Access to **Water Shut Off** in case of emergency
- [ ] YES [ ] NO Access to **Gas Shut Off** in case of emergency

Notes:

CONTRACTS

[ ] YES [ ] NO **Contract:** Has the location owner sign the contract/location release?

[ ] YES [ ] NO **Insurance:** Does the production insurance cover the location?

Dates needed: _____   Total number of days: _____   Total cost: _____

Contact person: _____

Phone: _____   email: _____

Project:

Director:

Producer:

Location scout:

Scene: Scene Number:

Location name:

Address:

STORY

☐ **Storytelling:** Does the location meet the scene requirements and fit the director's tone?

☐ **Anachronism:** Does the setting fit the time period and story setting?

Notes:

SIGHT

○ interior   ○ exterior

YES NO **Wide Shot test:** Wide frame acceptable?

YES NO **Wide Shot test:** Any problematicvisual elements in the frame?

YES NO **360 test:** Are there any problematic directions that should be avoided?

YES NO **Commercial clearance:** Any properties that require commercial clearance?

YES NO **Indoor staging:** Does the crew, cast and gear fit inside?

YES NO **VFX Need:** Would anything need to be removed or added in post?

YES NO **Indoor staging:** Any special production design needs?

YES NO **Sunlight:** Any sunlight consideration?

○ morning   ○ noon   ○ afternoon   ○ evening   ○ night

Notes:

SOUND

YES NO **HVAC:** Can you turn off the heating, ventilation and air conditioning unit?

YES NO **Refrigerators:** Can you turn off any noisy ? appliances or refrigerators?

YES NO **Reverberation:** Can you record clean dialog?

YES NO **Reverberation:** Do you need to dampen echoes in the space?

Notes:

SURROUNDINGS

YES	NO	**Roads & Traffic:** Noise or continuity issues from vehicles or pedestrians?
YES	NO	**Schools:** Noise or other issues connected with students?
YES	NO	**Playgrounds:** Will noise affected the sound or will people be in the frame?
YES	NO	**Factories:** Any noise generated from the machines or any road issues?
YES	NO	**Gas station:** Any noise or traffic issues?
YES	NO	**Parking:** Is there sufficient parking for talent, crew, and production vehicles?

YES	NO	**Airports:** Noise or activity and traffic issues and concerns?
YES	NO	**Air traffic:** Any significant air traffic overhead and sound concerns?
YES	NO	**Subway:** Will subway noise fit to the scene? Will it affect sound recording?
YES	NO	**Subway:** Will subway noise fit to the scene? Will it affect sound recording?
YES	NO	**Train station:** Will train noise fit in the scene? Any train appear in the frame?
YES	NO	**Staging Talent:** Is there a quiet place dedicated for talent, extras, crew?
YES	NO	**Restrooms:** Is there a enough restrooms for all?

Notes:

WEATHER

| YES | NO | **Temperature:** Is there temperature control? |

| YES | NO | **Rain / snow:** Will precipitation have a potential impact on the shoot? |
| YES | NO | **Indoor:** Will sound from precipitation have a potential impact on the shoot? |

Notes:

POWER

[ ] How many accessible outlets?

| YES | NO | **Access:** Does the electrical crew has access to the circuit breaker box? |
| YES | NO | **Hair and makeup:** Is there a dedicated space and breaker for Hair & Makeup? |

FACILITIES

[ ] How many people on set to every available bathroom?

| YES | NO | Access to **Water Shut Off** in case of emergency |
| YES | NO | Access to **Gas Shut Off** in case of emergency |

Notes:

CONTRACTS

| YES | NO | **Contract:** Has the location owner sign the contract/location release? |
| YES | NO | **Insurance:** Does the production insurance cover the location? |

Dates needed: Total number of days: Total cost:

Contact person:

Phone: email:

LOCATION SCOUTING CHECKLIST

Project:

Director:

Producer:

Location scout:

Scene: Scene Number:

Location name:

Address:

STORY

☐ **Storytelling:** Does the location meet the scene requirements and fit the director's tone?

☐ **Anachronism:** Does the setting fit the time period and story setting?

Notes:

SIGHT

○ interior   ○ exterior

YES NO **Wide Shot test:** Wide frame acceptable?

YES NO **Wide Shot test:** Any problematicvisual elements in the frame?

YES NO **360 test:** Are there any problematic directions that should be avoided?

YES NO **Commercial clearance:** Any properties that require commercial clearance?

YES NO **Indoor staging:** Does the crew, cast and gear fit inside?

YES NO **VFX Need:** Would anything need to be removed or added in post?

YES NO **Indoor staging:** Any special production design needs?

YES NO **Sunlight:** Any sunlight consideration?

○ morning ○ noon ○ afternoon ○ evening ○ night

Notes:

SOUND

YES NO **HVAC:** Can you turn off the heating, ventilation and air conditioning unit?

YES NO **Refrigerators:** Can you turn off any noisy ? appliances or refrigerators?

YES NO **Reverberation:** Can you record clean dialog?

YES NO **Reverberation:** Do you need to dampen echoes in the space?

Notes:

SURROUNDINGS

[YES] [NO] **Roads & Traffic:** Noise or continuity issues from vehicles or pedestrians?

[YES] [NO] **Schools:** Noise or other issues connected with students?

[YES] [NO] **Playgrounds:** Will noise affected the sound or will people be in the frame?

[YES] [NO] **Factories:** Any noise generated from the machines or any road issues?

[YES] [NO] **Gas station:** Any noise or traffic issues?

[YES] [NO] **Parking:** Is there sufficient parking for talent, crew, and production vehicles?

[YES] [NO] **Airports:** Noise or activity and traffic issues and concerns?

[YES] [NO] **Air traffic:** Any significant air traffic overhead and sound concerns?

[YES] [NO] **Subway:** Will subway noise fit to the scene? Will it affect sound recording?

[YES] [NO] **Subway:** Will subway noise fit to the scene? Will it affect sound recording?

[YES] [NO] **Train station:** Will train noise fit in the scene? Any train appear in the frame?

[YES] [NO] **Staging Talent:** Is there a quiet place dedicated for talent, extras, crew?

[YES] [NO] **Restrooms:** Is there a enough restrooms for all?

Notes:

WEATHER

[YES] [NO] **Temperature:** Is there temperature control?

[YES] [NO] **Rain / snow:** Will precipitation have a potential impact on the shoot?

[YES] [NO] **Indoor:** Will sound from precipitation have a potential impact on the shoot?

Notes:

POWER

[   ] How many accessible outlets?

[YES] [NO] **Access:** Does the electrical crew has access to the circuit breaker box?

[YES] [NO] **Hair and makeup:** Is there a dedicated space and breaker for Hair & Makeup?

FACILITIES

[   ] How many people on set to every available bathroom?

[YES] [NO] Access to **Water Shut Off** in case of emergency

[YES] [NO] Access to **Gas Shut Off** in case of emergency

Notes:

CONTRACTS

[YES] [NO] **Contract:** Has the location owner sign the contract/location release?

[YES] [NO] **Insurance:** Does the production insurance cover the location?

Dates needed: Total number of days: Total cost:

Contact person:

Phone: email:

Project:

Director:

Producer:

Location scout:

Scene: Scene Number:

Location name:

Address:

STORY

☐ **Storytelling:** Does the location meet the scene requirements and fit the director's tone?

☐ **Anachronism:** Does the setting fit the time period and story setting?

Notes:

SIGHT

○ interior   ○ exterior

☐ YES ☐ NO **Wide Shot test:** Wide frame acceptable?

☐ YES ☐ NO **Wide Shot test:** Any problematic visual elements in the frame?

☐ YES ☐ NO **360 test:** Are there any problematic directions that should be avoided?

☐ YES ☐ NO **Commercial clearance:** Any properties that require commercial clearance?

☐ YES ☐ NO **Indoor staging:** Does the crew, cast and gear fit inside?

☐ YES ☐ NO **VFX Need:** Would anything need to be removed or added in post?

☐ YES ☐ NO **Indoor staging:** Any special production design needs?

☐ YES ☐ NO **Sunlight:** Any sunlight consideration?

○ morning   ○ noon   ○ afternoon   ○ evening   ○ night

Notes:

SOUND

☐ YES ☐ NO **HVAC:** Can you turn off the heating, ventilation and air conditioning unit?

☐ YES ☐ NO **Refrigerators:** Can you turn off any noisy? appliances or refrigerators?

☐ YES ☐ NO **Reverberation:** Can you record clean dialog?

☐ YES ☐ NO **Reverberation:** Do you need to dampen echoes in the space?

Notes:

LOCATION SCOUTING CHECKLIST

SURROUNDINGS

[YES] [NO] Roads & Traffic: Noise or continuity issues from vehicles or pedestrians?

[YES] [NO] Schools: Noise or other issues connected with students?

[YES] [NO] Playgrounds: Will noise affected the sound or will people be in the frame?

[YES] [NO] Factories: Any noise generated from the machines or any road issues?

[YES] [NO] Gas station: Any noise or traffic issues?

[YES] [NO] Parking: Is there sufficient parking for talent, crew, and production vehicles?

[YES] [NO] Airports: Noise or activity and traffic issues and concerns?

[YES] [NO] Air traffic: Any significant air traffic overhead and sound concerns?

[YES] [NO] Subway: Will subway noise fit to the scene? Will it affect sound recording?

[YES] [NO] Subway: Will subway noise fit to the scene? Will it affect sound recording?

[YES] [NO] Train station: Will train noise fit in the scene? Any train appear in the frame?

[YES] [NO] Staging Talent: Is there a quiet place dedicated for talent, extras, crew?

[YES] [NO] Restrooms: Is there a enough restrooms for all?

Notes:

WEATHER

[YES] [NO] Temperature: Is there temperature control?

[YES] [NO] Rain / snow: Will precipitation have a potential impact on the shoot?

[YES] [NO] Indoor: Will sound from precipitation have a potential impact on the shoot?

Notes:

POWER

[ ] How many accessible outlets?

[YES] [NO] Access: Does the electrical crew has access to the circuit breaker box?

[YES] [NO] Hair and makeup: Is there a dedicated space and breaker for Hair & Makeup?

FACILITIES

[ ] How many people on set to every available bathroom?

[YES] [NO] Access to **Water Shut Off** in case of emergency

[YES] [NO] Access to **Gas Shut Off** in case of emergency

Notes:

CONTRACTS

[YES] [NO] Contract: Has the location owner sign the contract/location release?

[YES] [NO] Insurance: Does the production insurance cover the location?

Dates needed: _____   Total number of days: _____   Total cost: _____

Contact person: _____

Phone: _____   email: _____

LOCATION SCOUTING CHECKLIST

Project:

Director:

Producer:

Location scout:

Scene: Scene Number:

Location name:

Address:

STORY

☐ **Storytelling:** Does the location meet the scene requirements and fit the director's tone?

☐ **Anachronism:** Does the setting fit the time period and story setting?

Notes:

SIGHT

○ interior   ○ exterior

YES	NO	**Wide Shot test:** Wide frame acceptable?
YES	NO	**Wide Shot test:** Any problematicvisual elements in the frame?
YES	NO	**360 test:** Are there any problematic directions that should be avoided?
YES	NO	**Commercial clearance:** Any properties that require commercial clearance?

YES	NO	**Indoor staging:** Does the crew, cast and gear fit inside?
YES	NO	**VFX Need:** Would anything need to be removed or added in post?
YES	NO	**Indoor staging:** Any special production design needs?
YES	NO	**Sunlight:** Any sunlight consideration?

○ morning   ○ noon   ○ afternoon   ○ evening   ○ night

Notes:

SOUND

YES	NO	**HVAC:** Can you turn off the heating, ventilation and air conditioning unit?
YES	NO	**Refrigerators:** Can you turn off any noisy ? appliances or refrigerators?

YES	NO	**Reverberation:** Can you record clean dialog?
YES	NO	**Reverberation:** Do you need to dampen echoes in the space?

Notes:

LOCATION SCOUTING CHECKLIST

SURROUNDINGS

YES **NO** **Roads & Traffic:** Noise or continuity issues from vehicles or pedestrians?

YES **NO** **Schools:** Noise or other issues connected with students?

YES **NO** **Playgrounds:** Will noise affected the sound or will people be in the frame?

YES **NO** **Factories:** Any noise generated from the machines or any road issues?

YES **NO** **Gas station:** Any noise or traffic issues?

YES **NO** **Parking:** Is there sufficient parking for talent, crew, and production vehicles?

YES **NO** **Airports:** Noise or activity and traffic issues and concerns?

YES **NO** **Air traffic:** Any significant air traffic overhead and sound concerns?

YES **NO** **Subway:** Will subway noise fit to the scene? Will it affect sound recording?

YES **NO** **Subway:** Will subway noise fit to the scene? Will it affect sound recording?

YES **NO** **Train station:** Will train noise fit in the scene? Any train appear in the frame?

YES **NO** **Staging Talent:** Is there a quiet place dedicated for talent, extras, crew?

YES **NO** **Restrooms:** Is there a enough restrooms for all?

Notes:

WEATHER

YES **NO** **Temperature:** Is there temperature control?

YES **NO** **Rain / snow:** Will precipitation have a potential impact on the shoot?

YES **NO** **Indoor:** Will sound from precipitation have a potential impact on the shoot?

Notes:

POWER
[ ] How many accessible outlets?

YES **NO** **Access:** Does the electrical crew has access to the circuit breaker box?

YES **NO** **Hair and makeup:** Is there a dedicated space and breaker for Hair & Makeup?

FACILITIES
[ ] How many people on set to every available bathroom?

YES **NO** Access to **Water Shut Off** in case of emergency

YES **NO** Access to **Gas Shut Off** in case of emergency

Notes:

CONTRACTS
YES **NO** **Contract:** Has the location owner sign the contract/location release?

YES **NO** **Insurance:** Does the production insurance cover the location?

Dates needed: _____   Total number of days: _____   Total cost: _____

Contact person: _____

Phone: _____   email: _____

Project:

Director:

Producer:

Location scout:

Scene: Scene Number:

Location name:

Address:

STORY

☐ **Storytelling:** Does the location meet the scene requirements and fit the director's tone?

☐ **Anachronism:** Does the setting fit the time period and story setting?

Notes:

SIGHT

○ interior   ○ exterior

[YES] [NO] **Wide Shot test:** Wide frame acceptable?

[YES] [NO] **Wide Shot test:** Any problematicvisual elements in the frame?

[YES] [NO] **360 test:** Are there any problematic directions that should be avoided?

[YES] [NO] **Commercial clearance:** Any properties that require commercial clearance?

[YES] [NO] **Indoor staging:** Does the crew, cast and gear fit inside?

[YES] [NO] **VFX Need:** Would anything need to be removed or added in post?

[YES] [NO] **Indoor staging:** Any special production design needs?

[YES] [NO] **Sunlight:** Any sunlight consideration?

○ morning   ○ noon   ○ afternoon   ○ evening   ○ night

Notes:

SOUND

[YES] [NO] **HVAC:** Can you turn off the heating, ventilation and air conditioning unit?

[YES] [NO] **Refrigerators:** Can you turn off any noisy ? appliances or refrigerators?

[YES] [NO] **Reverberation:** Can you record clean dialog?

[YES] [NO] **Reverberation:** Do you need to dampen echoes in the space?

Notes:

LOCATION SCOUTING CHECKLIST

SURROUNDINGS

[YES] [NO] Roads & Traffic: Noise or continuity issues from vehicles or pedestrians?

[YES] [NO] Schools: Noise or other issues connected with students?

[YES] [NO] Playgrounds: Will noise affected the sound or will people be in the frame?

[YES] [NO] Factories: Any noise generated from the machines or any road issues?

[YES] [NO] Gas station: Any noise or traffic issues?

[YES] [NO] Parking: Is there sufficient parking for talent, crew, and production vehicles?

[YES] [NO] Airports: Noise or activity and traffic issues and concerns?

[YES] [NO] Air traffic: Any significant air traffic overhead and sound concerns?

[YES] [NO] Subway: Will subway noise fit to the scene? Will it affect sound recording?

[YES] [NO] Subway: Will subway noise fit to the scene? Will it affect sound recording?

[YES] [NO] Train station: Will train noise fit in the scene? Any train appear in the frame?

[YES] [NO] Staging Talent: Is there a quiet place dedicated for talent, extras, crew?

[YES] [NO] Restrooms: Is there a enough restrooms for all?

Notes:

WEATHER

[YES] [NO] Temperature: Is there temperature control?

[YES] [NO] Rain / snow: Will precipitation have a potential impact on the shoot?

[YES] [NO] Indoor: Will sound from precipitation have a potential impact on the shoot?

Notes:

POWER

[ ] How many accessible outlets?

[YES] [NO] Access: Does the electrical crew has access to the circuit breaker box?

[YES] [NO] Hair and makeup: Is there a dedicated space and breaker for Hair & Makeup?

FACILITIES

[ ] How many people on set to every available bathroom?

[YES] [NO] Access to **Water Shut Off** in case of emergency

[YES] [NO] Access to **Gas Shut Off** in case of emergency

Notes:

CONTRACTS

[YES] [NO] Contract: Has the location owner sign the contract/location release?

[YES] [NO] Insurance: Does the production insurance cover the location?

Dates needed: _____ Total number of days: _____ Total cost: _____

Contact person: _____

Phone: _____   email: _____

LOCATION SCOUTING CHECKLIST

Project:

Director:

Producer:

Location scout:

Scene: Scene Number:

Location name:

Address:

STORY

☐ **Storytelling:** Does the location meet the scene requirements and fit the director's tone?

☐ **Anachronism:** Does the setting fit the time period and story setting?

Notes:

SIGHT

○ interior   ○ exterior

[YES] [NO] **Wide Shot test:** Wide frame acceptable?

[YES] [NO] **Wide Shot test:** Any problematicvisual elements in the frame?

[YES] [NO] **360 test:** Are there any problematic directions that should be avoided?

[YES] [NO] **Commercial clearance:** Any properties that require commercial clearance?

[YES] [NO] **Indoor staging:** Does the crew, cast and gear fit inside?

[YES] [NO] **VFX Need:** Would anything need to be removed or added in post?

[YES] [NO] **Indoor staging:** Any special production design needs?

[YES] [NO] **Sunlight:** Any sunlight consideration?

○ morning   ○ noon   ○ afternoon   ○ evening   ○ night

Notes:

SOUND

[YES] [NO] **HVAC:** Can you turn off the heating, ventilation and air conditioning unit?

[YES] [NO] **Refrigerators:** Can you turn off any noisy ? appliances or refrigerators?

[YES] [NO] **Reverberation:** Can you record clean dialog?

[YES] [NO] **Reverberation:** Do you need to dampen echoes in the space?

Notes:

SURROUNDINGS

Roads & Traffic: Noise or continuity issues from vehicles or pedestrians? [YES] [NO]

Schools: Noise or other issues connected with students? [YES] [NO]

Playgrounds: Will noise affected the sound or will people be in the frame? [YES] [NO]

Factories: Any noise generated from the machines or any road issues? [YES] [NO]

Gas station: Any noise or traffic issues? [YES] [NO]

Parking: Is there sufficient parking for talent, crew, and production vehicles? [YES] [NO]

Airports: Noise or activity and traffic issues and concerns? [YES] [NO]

Air traffic: Any significant air traffic overhead and sound concerns? [YES] [NO]

Subway: Will subway noise fit to the scene? Will it affect sound recording? [YES] [NO]

Subway: Will subway noise fit to the scene? Will it affect sound recording? [YES] [NO]

Train station: Will train noise fit in the scene? Any train appear in the frame? [YES] [NO]

Staging Talent: Is there a quiet place dedicated for talent, extras, crew? [YES] [NO]

Restrooms: Is there a enough restrooms for all? [YES] [NO]

Notes:

WEATHER

Temperature: Is there temperature control? [YES] [NO]

Rain / snow: Will precipitation have a potential impact on the shoot? [YES] [NO]

Indoor: Will sound from precipitation have a potential impact on the shoot? [YES] [NO]

Notes:

POWER

How many accessible outlets? [ ]

Access: Does the electrical crew has access to the circuit breaker box? [YES] [NO]

Hair and makeup: Is there a dedicated space and breaker for Hair & Makeup? [YES] [NO]

FACILITIES

How many people on set to every available bathroom? [ ]

Access to **Water Shut Off** in case of emergency [YES] [NO]

Access to **Gas Shut Off** in case of emergency [YES] [NO]

Notes:

CONTRACTS

[YES] [NO] **Contract:** Has the location owner sign the contract/location release?

[YES] [NO] **Insurance:** Does the production insurance cover the location?

Dates needed: _____ Total number of days: _____ Total cost: _____

Contact person: _____

Phone: _____   email: _____

LOCATION SCOUTING CHECKLIST

Project:

Director:

Producer:

Location scout:

Scene: Scene Number:

Location name:

Address:

STORY

☐ **Storytelling:** Does the location meet the scene requirements and fit the director's tone?

☐ **Anachronism:** Does the setting fit the time period and story setting?

Notes:

SIGHT

○ interior   ○ exterior

[YES] [NO] **Wide Shot test:** Wide frame acceptable?

[YES] [NO] **Wide Shot test:** Any problematicvisual elements in the frame?

[YES] [NO] **360 test:** Are there any problematic directions that should be avoided?

[YES] [NO] **Commercial clearance:** Any properties that require commercial clearance?

[YES] [NO] **Indoor staging:** Does the crew, cast and gear fit inside?

[YES] [NO] **VFX Need:** Would anything need to be removed or added in post?

[YES] [NO] **Indoor staging:** Any special production design needs?

[YES] [NO] **Sunlight:** Any sunlight consideration?

○ morning   ○ noon   ○ afternoon   ○ evening   ○ night

Notes:

SOUND

[YES] [NO] **HVAC:** Can you turn off the heating, ventilation and air conditioning unit?

[YES] [NO] **Refrigerators:** Can you turn off any noisy ? appliances or refrigerators?

[YES] [NO] **Reverberation:** Can you record clean dialog?

[YES] [NO] **Reverberation:** Do you need to dampen echoes in the space?

Notes:

SURROUNDINGS

| YES | NO | Roads & Traffic: Noise or continuity issues from vehicles or pedestrians? |

| YES | NO | Schools: Noise or other issues connected with students? |

| YES | NO | Playgrounds: Will noise affected the sound or will people be in the frame? |

| YES | NO | Factories: Any noise generated from the machines or any road issues? |

| YES | NO | Gas station: Any noise or traffic issues? |

| YES | NO | Parking: Is there sufficient parking for talent, crew, and production vehicles? |

| YES | NO | Airports: Noise or activity and traffic issues and concerns? |

| YES | NO | Air traffic: Any significant air traffic overhead and sound concerns? |

| YES | NO | Subway: Will subway noise fit to the scene? Will it affect sound recording? |

| YES | NO | Subway: Will subway noise fit to the scene? Will it affect sound recording? |

| YES | NO | Train station: Will train noise fit in the scene? Any train appear in the frame? |

| YES | NO | Staging Talent: Is there a quiet place dedicated for talent, extras, crew? |

| YES | NO | Restrooms: Is there a enough restrooms for all? |

Notes:

WEATHER

| YES | NO | Temperature: Is there temperature control? |

| YES | NO | Rain / snow: Will precipitation have a potential impact on the shoot? |

| YES | NO | Indoor: Will sound from precipitation have a potential impact on the shoot? |

Notes:

POWER

How many accessible outlets?

| YES | NO | Access: Does the electrical crew has access to the circuit breaker box? |

| YES | NO | Hair and makeup: Is there a dedicated space and breaker for Hair & Makeup? |

FACILITIES

How many people on set to every available bathroom?

| YES | NO | Access to Water Shut Off in case of emergency |

| YES | NO | Access to Gas Shut Off in case of emergency |

Notes:

CONTRACTS

| YES | NO | Contract: Has the location owner sign the contract/location release? |

| YES | NO | Insurance: Does the production insurance cover the location? |

Dates needed: Total number of days: Total cost:

Contact person:

Phone: email:

LOCATION SCOUTING CHECKLIST

Project:

Director:

Producer:

Location scout:

Scene: Scene Number:

Location name:

Address:

STORY

☐ **Storytelling:** Does the location meet the scene requirements and fit the director's tone?

☐ **Anachronism:** Does the setting fit the time period and story setting?

Notes:

SIGHT

○ interior   ○ exterior

[YES] [NO] **Wide Shot test:** Wide frame acceptable?

[YES] [NO] **Wide Shot test:** Any problematicvisual elements in the frame?

[YES] [NO] **360 test:** Are there any problematic directions that should be avoided?

[YES] [NO] **Commercial clearance:** Any properties that require commercial clearance?

[YES] [NO] **Indoor staging:** Does the crew, cast and gear fit inside?

[YES] [NO] **VFX Need:** Would anything need to be removed or added in post?

[YES] [NO] **Indoor staging:** Any special production design needs?

[YES] [NO] **Sunlight:** Any sunlight consideration?

○ morning   ○ noon   ○ afternoon   ○ evening   ○ night

Notes:

SOUND

[YES] [NO] **HVAC:** Can you turn off the heating, ventilation and air conditioning unit?

[YES] [NO] **Refrigerators:** Can you turn off any noisy ? appliances or refrigerators?

[YES] [NO] **Reverberation:** Can you record clean dialog?

[YES] [NO] **Reverberation:** Do you need to dampen echoes in the space?

Notes:

SURROUNDINGS

YES	NO	**Roads & Traffic:** Noise or continuity issues from vehicles or pedestrians?
YES	NO	**Schools:** Noise or other issues connected with students?
YES	NO	**Playgrounds:** Will noise affected the sound or will people be in the frame?
YES	NO	**Factories:** Any noise generated from the machines or any road issues?
YES	NO	**Gas station:** Any noise or traffic issues?
YES	NO	**Parking:** Is there sufficient parking for talent, crew, and production vehicles?

YES	NO	**Airports:** Noise or activity and traffic issues and concerns?
YES	NO	**Air traffic:** Any significant air traffic overhead and sound concerns?
YES	NO	**Subway:** Will subway noise fit to the scene? Will it affect sound recording?
YES	NO	**Subway:** Will subway noise fit to the scene? Will it affect sound recording?
YES	NO	**Train station:** Will train noise fit in the scene? Any train appear in the frame?
YES	NO	**Staging Talent:** Is there a quiet place dedicated for talent, extras, crew?
YES	NO	**Restrooms:** Is there a enough restrooms for all?

Notes:

WEATHER

YES	NO	**Temperature:** Is there temperature control?

YES	NO	**Rain / snow:** Will precipitation have a potential impact on the shoot?
YES	NO	**Indoor:** Will sound from precipitation have a potential impact on the shoot?

Notes:

POWER

[   ] How many accessible outlets?

YES	NO	**Access:** Does the electrical crew has access to the circuit breaker box?
YES	NO	**Hair and makeup:** Is there a dedicated space and breaker for Hair & Makeup?

FACILITIES

[   ] How many people on set to every available bathroom?

YES	NO	Access to **Water Shut Off** in case of emergency
YES	NO	Access to **Gas Shut Off** in case of emergency

Notes:

CONTRACTS

YES	NO	**Contract:** Has the location owner sign the contract/location release?

YES	NO	**Insurance:** Does the production insurance cover the location?

Dates needed: Total number of days: Total cost:

Contact person:

Phone: email:

LOCATION SCOUTING CHECKLIST

Project:

Director:

Producer:

Location scout:

Scene: Scene Number:

Location name:

Address:

STORY

☐ **Storytelling:** Does the location meet the scene requirements and fit the director's tone?

☐ **Anachronism:** Does the setting fit the time period and story setting?

Notes:

SIGHT

○ interior   ○ exterior

☐ YES ☐ NO **Wide Shot test:** Wide frame acceptable?

☐ YES ☐ NO **Wide Shot test:** Any problematicvisual elements in the frame?

☐ YES ☐ NO **360 test:** Are there any problematic directions that should be avoided?

☐ YES ☐ NO **Commercial clearance:** Any properties that require commercial clearance?

☐ YES ☐ NO **Indoor staging:** Does the crew, cast and gear fit inside?

☐ YES ☐ NO **VFX Need:** Would anything need to be removed or added in post?

☐ YES ☐ NO **Indoor staging:** Any special production design needs?

☐ YES ☐ NO **Sunlight:** Any sunlight consideration?

○ morning   ○ noon   ○ afternoon   ○ evening   ○ night

Notes:

SOUND

☐ YES ☐ NO **HVAC:** Can you turn off the heating, ventilation and air conditioning unit?

☐ YES ☐ NO **Refrigerators:** Can you turn off any noisy ? appliances or refrigerators?

☐ YES ☐ NO **Reverberation:** Can you record clean dialog?

☐ YES ☐ NO **Reverberation:** Do you need to dampen echoes in the space?

Notes:

SURROUNDINGS

YES	NO	**Roads & Traffic:** Noise or continuity issues from vehicles or pedestrians?
YES	NO	**Schools:** Noise or other issues connected with students?
YES	NO	**Playgrounds:** Will noise affected the sound or will people be in the frame?
YES	NO	**Factories:** Any noise generated from the machines or any road issues?
YES	NO	**Gas station:** Any noise or traffic issues?
YES	NO	**Parking:** Is there sufficient parking for talent, crew, and production vehicles?

YES	NO	**Airports:** Noise or activity and traffic issues and concerns?
YES	NO	**Air traffic:** Any significant air traffic overhead and sound concerns?
YES	NO	**Subway:** Will subway noise fit to the scene? Will it affect sound recording?
YES	NO	**Subway:** Will subway noise fit to the scene? Will it affect sound recording?
YES	NO	**Train station:** Will train noise fit in the scene? Any train appear in the frame?
YES	NO	**Staging Talent:** Is there a quiet place dedicated for talent, extras, crew?
YES	NO	**Restrooms:** Is there a enough restrooms for all?

Notes:

WEATHER

| YES | NO | **Temperature:** Is there temperature control? |

| YES | NO | **Rain / snow:** Will precipitation have a potential impact on the shoot? |
| YES | NO | **Indoor:** Will sound from precipitation have a potential impact on the shoot? |

Notes:

POWER
[ ] How many accessible outlets?

| YES | NO | **Access:** Does the electrical crew has access to the circuit breaker box? |
| YES | NO | **Hair and makeup:** Is there a dedicated space and breaker for Hair & Makeup? |

FACILITIES
[ ] How many people on set to every available bathroom?

| YES | NO | Access to **Water Shut Off** in case of emergency |
| YES | NO | Access to **Gas Shut Off** in case of emergency |

Notes:

CONTRACTS
| YES | NO | **Contract:** Has the location owner sign the contract/location release? |
| YES | NO | **Insurance:** Does the production insurance cover the location? |

Dates needed: _____ Total number of days: _____ Total cost: _____

Contact person: _____

Phone: _____ email: _____

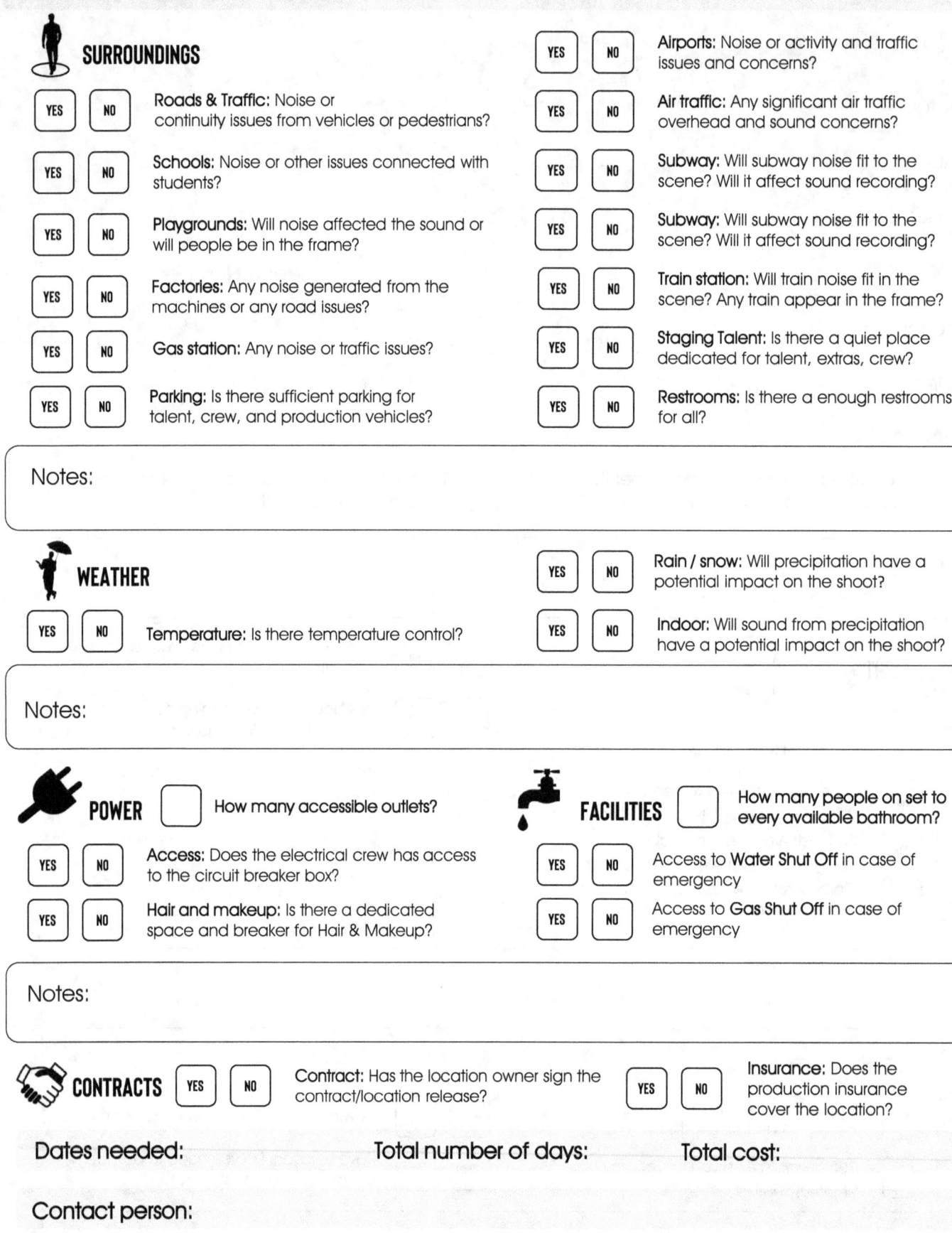

Project:

Director:

Producer:

Location scout:

Scene: Scene Number:

Location name:

Address:

STORY

☐ **Storytelling:** Does the location meet the scene requirements and fit the director's tone?

☐ **Anachronism:** Does the setting fit the time period and story setting?

Notes:

SIGHT

◯ interior   ◯ exterior

[YES] [NO] **Wide Shot test:** Wide frame acceptable?

[YES] [NO] **Wide Shot test:** Any problematicvisual elements in the frame?

[YES] [NO] **360 test:** Are there any problematic directions that should be avoided?

[YES] [NO] **Commercial clearance:** Any properties that require commercial clearance?

[YES] [NO] **Indoor staging:** Does the crew, cast and gear fit inside?

[YES] [NO] **VFX Need:** Would anything need to be removed or added in post?

[YES] [NO] **Indoor staging:** Any special production design needs?

[YES] [NO] **Sunlight:** Any sunlight consideration?

◯ morning   ◯ noon   ◯ afternoon   ◯ evening   ◯ night

Notes:

SOUND

[YES] [NO] **HVAC:** Can you turn off the heating, ventilation and air conditioning unit?

[YES] [NO] **Refrigerators:** Can you turn off any noisy ? appliances or refrigerators?

[YES] [NO] **Reverberation:** Can you record clean dialog?

[YES] [NO] **Reverberation:** Do you need to dampen echoes in the space?

Notes:

SURROUNDINGS

[YES] [NO] **Roads & Traffic:** Noise or continuity issues from vehicles or pedestrians?

[YES] [NO] **Schools:** Noise or other issues connected with students?

[YES] [NO] **Playgrounds:** Will noise affected the sound or will people be in the frame?

[YES] [NO] **Factories:** Any noise generated from the machines or any road issues?

[YES] [NO] **Gas station:** Any noise or traffic issues?

[YES] [NO] **Parking:** Is there sufficient parking for talent, crew, and production vehicles?

[YES] [NO] **Airports:** Noise or activity and traffic issues and concerns?

[YES] [NO] **Air traffic:** Any significant air traffic overhead and sound concerns?

[YES] [NO] **Subway:** Will subway noise fit to the scene? Will it affect sound recording?

[YES] [NO] **Subway:** Will subway noise fit to the scene? Will it affect sound recording?

[YES] [NO] **Train station:** Will train noise fit in the scene? Any train appear in the frame?

[YES] [NO] **Staging Talent:** Is there a quiet place dedicated for talent, extras, crew?

[YES] [NO] **Restrooms:** Is there a enough restrooms for all?

Notes:

WEATHER

[YES] [NO] **Temperature:** Is there temperature control?

[YES] [NO] **Rain / snow:** Will precipitation have a potential impact on the shoot?

[YES] [NO] **Indoor:** Will sound from precipitation have a potential impact on the shoot?

Notes:

POWER

[ ] How many accessible outlets?

[YES] [NO] **Access:** Does the electrical crew has access to the circuit breaker box?

[YES] [NO] **Hair and makeup:** Is there a dedicated space and breaker for Hair & Makeup?

FACILITIES

[ ] How many people on set to every available bathroom?

[YES] [NO] Access to **Water Shut Off** in case of emergency

[YES] [NO] Access to **Gas Shut Off** in case of emergency

Notes:

CONTRACTS

[YES] [NO] **Contract:** Has the location owner sign the contract/location release?

[YES] [NO] **Insurance:** Does the production insurance cover the location?

Dates needed: Total number of days: Total cost:

Contact person:

Phone: email:

LOCATION SCOUTING CHECKLIST

Project:

Director:

Producer:

Location scout:

Scene: Scene Number:

Location name:

Address:

STORY

☐ **Storytelling:** Does the location meet the scene requirements and fit the director's tone?

☐ **Anachronism:** Does the setting fit the time period and story setting?

Notes:

SIGHT

○ interior   ○ exterior

YES	NO	**Wide Shot test:** Wide frame acceptable?
YES	NO	**Wide Shot test:** Any problematicvisual elements in the frame?
YES	NO	**360 test:** Are there any problematic directions that should be avoided?
YES	NO	**Commercial clearance:** Any properties that require commercial clearance?

YES	NO	**Indoor staging:** Does the crew, cast and gear fit inside?
YES	NO	**VFX Need:** Would anything need to be removed or added in post?
YES	NO	**Indoor staging:** Any special production design needs?
YES	NO	**Sunlight:** Any sunlight consideration?

○ morning   ○ noon   ○ afternoon   ○ evening   ○ night

Notes:

SOUND

| YES | NO | **HVAC:** Can you turn off the heating, ventilation and air conditioning unit? |
| YES | NO | **Refrigerators:** Can you turn off any noisy ? appliances or refrigerators? |

| YES | NO | **Reverberation:** Can you record clean dialog? |
| YES | NO | **Reverberation:** Do you need to dampen echoes in the space? |

Notes:

SURROUNDINGS

[YES] [NO] **Roads & Traffic:** Noise or continuity issues from vehicles or pedestrians?

[YES] [NO] **Schools:** Noise or other issues connected with students?

[YES] [NO] **Playgrounds:** Will noise affected the sound or will people be in the frame?

[YES] [NO] **Factories:** Any noise generated from the machines or any road issues?

[YES] [NO] **Gas station:** Any noise or traffic issues?

[YES] [NO] **Parking:** Is there sufficient parking for talent, crew, and production vehicles?

[YES] [NO] **Airports:** Noise or activity and traffic issues and concerns?

[YES] [NO] **Air traffic:** Any significant air traffic overhead and sound concerns?

[YES] [NO] **Subway:** Will subway noise fit to the scene? Will it affect sound recording?

[YES] [NO] **Subway:** Will subway noise fit to the scene? Will it affect sound recording?

[YES] [NO] **Train station:** Will train noise fit in the scene? Any train appear in the frame?

[YES] [NO] **Staging Talent:** Is there a quiet place dedicated for talent, extras, crew?

[YES] [NO] **Restrooms:** Is there a enough restrooms for all?

Notes:

WEATHER

[YES] [NO] **Temperature:** Is there temperature control?

[YES] [NO] **Rain / snow:** Will precipitation have a potential impact on the shoot?

[YES] [NO] **Indoor:** Will sound from precipitation have a potential impact on the shoot?

Notes:

POWER

[ ] How many accessible outlets?

[YES] [NO] **Access:** Does the electrical crew has access to the circuit breaker box?

[YES] [NO] **Hair and makeup:** Is there a dedicated space and breaker for Hair & Makeup?

FACILITIES

[ ] How many people on set to every available bathroom?

[YES] [NO] Access to **Water Shut Off** in case of emergency

[YES] [NO] Access to **Gas Shut Off** in case of emergency

Notes:

CONTRACTS

[YES] [NO] **Contract:** Has the location owner sign the contract/location release?

[YES] [NO] **Insurance:** Does the production insurance cover the location?

Dates needed: _____ Total number of days: _____ Total cost: _____

Contact person: _____

Phone: _____ email: _____

LOCATION SCOUTING CHECKLIST

Project:

Director:

Producer:

Location scout:

Scene: Scene Number:

Location name:

Address:

STORY

☐ **Storytelling:** Does the location meet the scene requirements and fit the director's tone?

☐ **Anachronism:** Does the setting fit the time period and story setting?

Notes:

SIGHT

◯ interior   ◯ exterior

[YES] [NO] **Wide Shot test:** Wide frame acceptable?

[YES] [NO] **Wide Shot test:** Any problematicvisual elements in the frame?

[YES] [NO] **360 test:** Are there any problematic directions that should be avoided?

[YES] [NO] **Commercial clearance:** Any properties that require commercial clearance?

[YES] [NO] **Indoor staging:** Does the crew, cast and gear fit inside?

[YES] [NO] **VFX Need:** Would anything need to be removed or added in post?

[YES] [NO] **Indoor staging:** Any special production design needs?

[YES] [NO] **Sunlight:** Any sunlight consideration?

◯ morning   ◯ noon   ◯ afternoon   ◯ evening   ◯ night

Notes:

SOUND

[YES] [NO] **HVAC:** Can you turn off the heating, ventilation and air conditioning unit?

[YES] [NO] **Refrigerators:** Can you turn off any noisy ? appliances or refrigerators?

[YES] [NO] **Reverberation:** Can you record clean dialog?

[YES] [NO] **Reverberation:** Do you need to dampen echoes in the space?

Notes:

SURROUNDINGS

[YES] [NO] **Roads & Traffic:** Noise or continuity issues from vehicles or pedestrians?

[YES] [NO] **Schools:** Noise or other issues connected with students?

[YES] [NO] **Playgrounds:** Will noise affected the sound or will people be in the frame?

[YES] [NO] **Factories:** Any noise generated from the machines or any road issues?

[YES] [NO] **Gas station:** Any noise or traffic issues?

[YES] [NO] **Parking:** Is there sufficient parking for talent, crew, and production vehicles?

[YES] [NO] **Airports:** Noise or activity and traffic issues and concerns?

[YES] [NO] **Air traffic:** Any significant air traffic overhead and sound concerns?

[YES] [NO] **Subway:** Will subway noise fit to the scene? Will it affect sound recording?

[YES] [NO] **Subway:** Will subway noise fit to the scene? Will it affect sound recording?

[YES] [NO] **Train station:** Will train noise fit in the scene? Any train appear in the frame?

[YES] [NO] **Staging Talent:** Is there a quiet place dedicated for talent, extras, crew?

[YES] [NO] **Restrooms:** Is there a enough restrooms for all?

Notes:

WEATHER

[YES] [NO] **Temperature:** Is there temperature control?

[YES] [NO] **Rain / snow:** Will precipitation have a potential impact on the shoot?

[YES] [NO] **Indoor:** Will sound from precipitation have a potential impact on the shoot?

Notes:

POWER

[ ] How many accessible outlets?

[YES] [NO] **Access:** Does the electrical crew has access to the circuit breaker box?

[YES] [NO] **Hair and makeup:** Is there a dedicated space and breaker for Hair & Makeup?

FACILITIES

[ ] How many people on set to every available bathroom?

[YES] [NO] Access to **Water Shut Off** in case of emergency

[YES] [NO] Access to **Gas Shut Off** in case of emergency

Notes:

CONTRACTS

[YES] [NO] **Contract:** Has the location owner sign the contract/location release?

[YES] [NO] **Insurance:** Does the production insurance cover the location?

Dates needed: _____   Total number of days: _____   Total cost: _____

Contact person: _____

Phone: _____   email: _____

LOCATION SCOUTING CHECKLIST

Project:

Director:

Producer:

Location scout:

Scene: Scene Number:

Location name:

Address:

STORY

☐ **Storytelling:** Does the location meet the scene requirements and fit the director's tone?

☐ **Anachronism:** Does the setting fit the time period and story setting?

Notes:

SIGHT

○ interior   ○ exterior

[YES] [NO] **Wide Shot test:** Wide frame acceptable?

[YES] [NO] **Wide Shot test:** Any problematicvisual elements in the frame?

[YES] [NO] **360 test:** Are there any problematic directions that should be avoided?

[YES] [NO] **Commercial clearance:** Any properties that require commercial clearance?

[YES] [NO] **Indoor staging:** Does the crew, cast and gear fit inside?

[YES] [NO] **VFX Need:** Would anything need to be removed or added in post?

[YES] [NO] **Indoor staging:** Any special production design needs?

[YES] [NO] **Sunlight:** Any sunlight consideration?

○ morning   ○ noon   ○ afternoon   ○ evening   ○ night

Notes:

SOUND

[YES] [NO] **HVAC:** Can you turn off the heating, ventilation and air conditioning unit?

[YES] [NO] **Refrigerators:** Can you turn off any noisy ? appliances or refrigerators?

[YES] [NO] **Reverberation:** Can you record clean dialog?

[YES] [NO] **Reverberation:** Do you need to dampen echoes in the space?

Notes:

SURROUNDINGS

[YES] [NO] **Roads & Traffic:** Noise or continuity issues from vehicles or pedestrians?

[YES] [NO] **Schools:** Noise or other issues connected with students?

[YES] [NO] **Playgrounds:** Will noise affected the sound or will people be in the frame?

[YES] [NO] **Factories:** Any noise generated from the machines or any road issues?

[YES] [NO] **Gas station:** Any noise or traffic issues?

[YES] [NO] **Parking:** Is there sufficient parking for talent, crew, and production vehicles?

[YES] [NO] **Airports:** Noise or activity and traffic issues and concerns?

[YES] [NO] **Air traffic:** Any significant air traffic overhead and sound concerns?

[YES] [NO] **Subway:** Will subway noise fit to the scene? Will it affect sound recording?

[YES] [NO] **Subway:** Will subway noise fit to the scene? Will it affect sound recording?

[YES] [NO] **Train station:** Will train noise fit in the scene? Any train appear in the frame?

[YES] [NO] **Staging Talent:** Is there a quiet place dedicated for talent, extras, crew?

[YES] [NO] **Restrooms:** Is there a enough restrooms for all?

Notes:

WEATHER

[YES] [NO] **Temperature:** Is there temperature control?

[YES] [NO] **Rain / snow:** Will precipitation have a potential impact on the shoot?

[YES] [NO] **Indoor:** Will sound from precipitation have a potential impact on the shoot?

Notes:

POWER

[ ] How many accessible outlets?

[YES] [NO] **Access:** Does the electrical crew has access to the circuit breaker box?

[YES] [NO] **Hair and makeup:** Is there a dedicated space and breaker for Hair & Makeup?

FACILITIES

[ ] How many people on set to every available bathroom?

[YES] [NO] Access to **Water Shut Off** in case of emergency

[YES] [NO] Access to **Gas Shut Off** in case of emergency

Notes:

CONTRACTS

[YES] [NO] **Contract:** Has the location owner sign the contract/location release?

[YES] [NO] **Insurance:** Does the production insurance cover the location?

Dates needed: Total number of days: Total cost:

Contact person:

Phone: email:

LOCATION SCOUTING CHECKLIST

Project:

Director:

Producer:

Location scout:

Scene: Scene Number:

Location name:

Address:

STORY

☐ **Storytelling:** Does the location meet the scene requirements and fit the director's tone?

☐ **Anachronism:** Does the setting fit the time period and story setting?

Notes:

SIGHT

◯ interior   ◯ exterior

[YES] [NO] **Wide Shot test:** Wide frame acceptable?

[YES] [NO] **Wide Shot test:** Any problematicvisual elements in the frame?

[YES] [NO] **360 test:** Are there any problematic directions that should be avoided?

[YES] [NO] **Commercial clearance:** Any properties that require commercial clearance?

[YES] [NO] **Indoor staging:** Does the crew, cast and gear fit inside?

[YES] [NO] **VFX Need:** Would anything need to be removed or added in post?

[YES] [NO] **Indoor staging:** Any special production design needs?

[YES] [NO] **Sunlight:** Any sunlight consideration?

◯ morning   ◯ noon   ◯ afternoon   ◯ evening   ◯ night

Notes:

SOUND

[YES] [NO] **HVAC:** Can you turn off the heating, ventilation and air conditioning unit?

[YES] [NO] **Refrigerators:** Can you turn off any noisy ? appliances or refrigerators?

[YES] [NO] **Reverberation:** Can you record clean dialog?

[YES] [NO] **Reverberation:** Do you need to dampen echoes in the space?

Notes:

SURROUNDINGS

[YES] [NO] **Roads & Traffic:** Noise or continuity issues from vehicles or pedestrians?

[YES] [NO] **Schools:** Noise or other issues connected with students?

[YES] [NO] **Playgrounds:** Will noise affected the sound or will people be in the frame?

[YES] [NO] **Factories:** Any noise generated from the machines or any road issues?

[YES] [NO] **Gas station:** Any noise or traffic issues?

[YES] [NO] **Parking:** Is there sufficient parking for talent, crew, and production vehicles?

[YES] [NO] **Airports:** Noise or activity and traffic issues and concerns?

[YES] [NO] **Air traffic:** Any significant air traffic overhead and sound concerns?

[YES] [NO] **Subway:** Will subway noise fit to the scene? Will it affect sound recording?

[YES] [NO] **Subway:** Will subway noise fit to the scene? Will it affect sound recording?

[YES] [NO] **Train station:** Will train noise fit in the scene? Any train appear in the frame?

[YES] [NO] **Staging Talent:** Is there a quiet place dedicated for talent, extras, crew?

[YES] [NO] **Restrooms:** Is there a enough restrooms for all?

Notes:

WEATHER

[YES] [NO] **Temperature:** Is there temperature control?

[YES] [NO] **Rain / snow:** Will precipitation have a potential impact on the shoot?

[YES] [NO] **Indoor:** Will sound from precipitation have a potential impact on the shoot?

Notes:

POWER

[ ] How many accessible outlets?

[YES] [NO] **Access:** Does the electrical crew has access to the circuit breaker box?

[YES] [NO] **Hair and makeup:** Is there a dedicated space and breaker for Hair & Makeup?

FACILITIES

[ ] How many people on set to every available bathroom?

[YES] [NO] Access to **Water Shut Off** in case of emergency

[YES] [NO] Access to **Gas Shut Off** in case of emergency

Notes:

CONTRACTS

[YES] [NO] **Contract:** Has the location owner sign the contract/location release?

[YES] [NO] **Insurance:** Does the production insurance cover the location?

Dates needed: Total number of days: Total cost:

Contact person:

Phone: email:

LOCATION SCOUTING CHECKLIST

Project:

Director:

Producer:

Location scout:

Scene: Scene Number:

Location name:

Address:

STORY

☐ **Storytelling:** Does the location meet the scene requirements and fit the director's tone?

☐ **Anachronism:** Does the setting fit the time period and story setting?

Notes:

SIGHT

○ interior   ○ exterior

[YES] [NO] **Wide Shot test:** Wide frame acceptable?

[YES] [NO] **Wide Shot test:** Any problematicvisual elements in the frame?

[YES] [NO] **360 test:** Are there any problematic directions that should be avoided?

[YES] [NO] **Commercial clearance:** Any properties that require commercial clearance?

[YES] [NO] **Indoor staging:** Does the crew, cast and gear fit inside?

[YES] [NO] **VFX Need:** Would anything need to be removed or added in post?

[YES] [NO] **Indoor staging:** Any special production design needs?

[YES] [NO] **Sunlight:** Any sunlight consideration?

○ morning   ○ noon   ○ afternoon   ○ evening   ○ night

Notes:

SOUND

[YES] [NO] **HVAC:** Can you turn off the heating, ventilation and air conditioning unit?

[YES] [NO] **Refrigerators:** Can you turn off any noisy ? appliances or refrigerators?

[YES] [NO] **Reverberation:** Can you record clean dialog?

[YES] [NO] **Reverberation:** Do you need to dampen echoes in the space?

Notes:

SURROUNDINGS

[YES] [NO] **Roads & Traffic:** Noise or continuity issues from vehicles or pedestrians?

[YES] [NO] **Schools:** Noise or other issues connected with students?

[YES] [NO] **Playgrounds:** Will noise affected the sound or will people be in the frame?

[YES] [NO] **Factories:** Any noise generated from the machines or any road issues?

[YES] [NO] **Gas station:** Any noise or traffic issues?

[YES] [NO] **Parking:** Is there sufficient parking for talent, crew, and production vehicles?

[YES] [NO] **Airports:** Noise or activity and traffic issues and concerns?

[YES] [NO] **Air traffic:** Any significant air traffic overhead and sound concerns?

[YES] [NO] **Subway:** Will subway noise fit to the scene? Will it affect sound recording?

[YES] [NO] **Subway:** Will subway noise fit to the scene? Will it affect sound recording?

[YES] [NO] **Train station:** Will train noise fit in the scene? Any train appear in the frame?

[YES] [NO] **Staging Talent:** Is there a quiet place dedicated for talent, extras, crew?

[YES] [NO] **Restrooms:** Is there a enough restrooms for all?

Notes:

WEATHER

[YES] [NO] **Temperature:** Is there temperature control?

[YES] [NO] **Rain / snow:** Will precipitation have a potential impact on the shoot?

[YES] [NO] **Indoor:** Will sound from precipitation have a potential impact on the shoot?

Notes:

POWER

[ ] How many accessible outlets?

[YES] [NO] **Access:** Does the electrical crew has access to the circuit breaker box?

[YES] [NO] **Hair and makeup:** Is there a dedicated space and breaker for Hair & Makeup?

FACILITIES

[ ] How many people on set to every available bathroom?

[YES] [NO] Access to **Water Shut Off** in case of emergency

[YES] [NO] Access to **Gas Shut Off** in case of emergency

Notes:

CONTRACTS

[YES] [NO] **Contract:** Has the location owner sign the contract/location release?

[YES] [NO] **Insurance:** Does the production insurance cover the location?

Dates needed: **Total number of days:**   **Total cost:**

Contact person:

Phone: **email:**

LOCATION SCOUTING CHECKLIST

Project:

Director:

Producer:

Location scout:

Scene: Scene Number:

Location name:

Address:

STORY

☐ **Storytelling:** Does the location meet the scene requirements and fit the director's tone?

☐ **Anachronism:** Does the setting fit the time period and story setting?

Notes:

SIGHT

◯ interior   ◯ exterior

[YES] [NO] **Wide Shot test:** Wide frame acceptable?

[YES] [NO] **Wide Shot test:** Any problematic visual elements in the frame?

[YES] [NO] **360 test:** Are there any problematic directions that should be avoided?

[YES] [NO] **Commercial clearance:** Any properties that require commercial clearance?

[YES] [NO] **Indoor staging:** Does the crew, cast and gear fit inside?

[YES] [NO] **VFX Need:** Would anything need to be removed or added in post?

[YES] [NO] **Indoor staging:** Any special production design needs?

[YES] [NO] **Sunlight:** Any sunlight consideration?

◯ morning   ◯ noon   ◯ afternoon   ◯ evening   ◯ night

Notes:

SOUND

[YES] [NO] **HVAC:** Can you turn off the heating, ventilation and air conditioning unit?

[YES] [NO] **Refrigerators:** Can you turn off any noisy ? appliances or refrigerators?

[YES] [NO] **Reverberation:** Can you record clean dialog?

[YES] [NO] **Reverberation:** Do you need to dampen echoes in the space?

Notes:

SURROUNDINGS

YES NO **Roads & Traffic:** Noise or continuity issues from vehicles or pedestrians?

YES NO **Schools:** Noise or other issues connected with students?

YES NO **Playgrounds:** Will noise affected the sound or will people be in the frame?

YES NO **Factories:** Any noise generated from the machines or any road issues?

YES NO **Gas station:** Any noise or traffic issues?

YES NO **Parking:** Is there sufficient parking for talent, crew, and production vehicles?

YES NO **Airports:** Noise or activity and traffic issues and concerns?

YES NO **Air traffic:** Any significant air traffic overhead and sound concerns?

YES NO **Subway:** Will subway noise fit to the scene? Will it affect sound recording?

YES NO **Subway:** Will subway noise fit to the scene? Will it affect sound recording?

YES NO **Train station:** Will train noise fit in the scene? Any train appear in the frame?

YES NO **Staging Talent:** Is there a quiet place dedicated for talent, extras, crew?

YES NO **Restrooms:** Is there a enough restrooms for all?

Notes:

WEATHER

YES NO **Temperature:** Is there temperature control?

YES NO **Rain / snow:** Will precipitation have a potential impact on the shoot?

YES NO **Indoor:** Will sound from precipitation have a potential impact on the shoot?

Notes:

POWER

[ ] How many accessible outlets?

YES NO **Access:** Does the electrical crew has access to the circuit breaker box?

YES NO **Hair and makeup:** Is there a dedicated space and breaker for Hair & Makeup?

FACILITIES

[ ] How many people on set to every available bathroom?

YES NO Access to **Water Shut Off** in case of emergency

YES NO Access to **Gas Shut Off** in case of emergency

Notes:

CONTRACTS

YES NO **Contract:** Has the location owner sign the contract/location release?

YES NO **Insurance:** Does the production insurance cover the location?

Dates needed:

Total number of days:

Total cost:

Contact person:

Phone:

email:

LOCATION SCOUTING CHECKLIST

Project:

Director:

Producer:

Location scout:

Scene: Scene Number:

Location name:

Address:

STORY

☐ **Storytelling:** Does the location meet the scene requirements and fit the director's tone?

☐ **Anachronism:** Does the setting fit the time period and story setting?

Notes:

SIGHT

○ interior   ○ exterior

☐ YES ☐ NO **Wide Shot test:** Wide frame acceptable?

☐ YES ☐ NO **Wide Shot test:** Any problematicvisual elements in the frame?

☐ YES ☐ NO **360 test:** Are there any problematic directions that should be avoided?

☐ YES ☐ NO **Commercial clearance:** Any properties that require commercial clearance?

☐ YES ☐ NO **Indoor staging:** Does the crew, cast and gear fit inside?

☐ YES ☐ NO **VFX Need:** Would anything need to be removed or added in post?

☐ YES ☐ NO **Indoor staging:** Any special production design needs?

☐ YES ☐ NO **Sunlight:** Any sunlight consideration?

○ morning   ○ noon   ○ afternoon   ○ evening   ○ night

Notes:

SOUND

☐ YES ☐ NO **HVAC:** Can you turn off the heating, ventilation and air conditioning unit?

☐ YES ☐ NO **Refrigerators:** Can you turn off any noisy ? appliances or refrigerators?

☐ YES ☐ NO **Reverberation:** Can you record clean dialog?

☐ YES ☐ NO **Reverberation:** Do you need to dampen echoes in the space?

Notes:

SURROUNDINGS

YES	NO	**Roads & Traffic:** Noise or continuity issues from vehicles or pedestrians?
YES	NO	**Schools:** Noise or other issues connected with students?
YES	NO	**Playgrounds:** Will noise affected the sound or will people be in the frame?
YES	NO	**Factories:** Any noise generated from the machines or any road issues?
YES	NO	**Gas station:** Any noise or traffic issues?
YES	NO	**Parking:** Is there sufficient parking for talent, crew, and production vehicles?

YES	NO	**Airports:** Noise or activity and traffic issues and concerns?
YES	NO	**Air traffic:** Any significant air traffic overhead and sound concerns?
YES	NO	**Subway:** Will subway noise fit to the scene? Will it affect sound recording?
YES	NO	**Subway:** Will subway noise fit to the scene? Will it affect sound recording?
YES	NO	**Train station:** Will train noise fit in the scene? Any train appear in the frame?
YES	NO	**Staging Talent:** Is there a quiet place dedicated for talent, extras, crew?
YES	NO	**Restrooms:** Is there a enough restrooms for all?

Notes:

WEATHER

| YES | NO | **Temperature:** Is there temperature control? |

| YES | NO | **Rain / snow:** Will precipitation have a potential impact on the shoot? |
| YES | NO | **Indoor:** Will sound from precipitation have a potential impact on the shoot? |

Notes:

POWER

[ ] How many accessible outlets?

| YES | NO | **Access:** Does the electrical crew has access to the circuit breaker box? |
| YES | NO | **Hair and makeup:** Is there a dedicated space and breaker for Hair & Makeup? |

FACILITIES

[ ] How many people on set to every available bathroom?

| YES | NO | Access to **Water Shut Off** in case of emergency |
| YES | NO | Access to **Gas Shut Off** in case of emergency |

Notes:

CONTRACTS

| YES | NO | **Contract:** Has the location owner sign the contract/location release? |
| YES | NO | **Insurance:** Does the production insurance cover the location? |

Dates needed: Total number of days: Total cost:

Contact person:

Phone: email:

LOCATION SCOUTING CHECKLIST

Project:

Director:

Producer:

Location scout:

Scene: Scene Number:

Location name:

Address:

STORY

☐ **Storytelling:** Does the location meet the scene requirements and fit the director's tone?

☐ **Anachronism:** Does the setting fit the time period and story setting?

Notes:

SIGHT

○ interior   ○ exterior

YES NO **Wide Shot test:** Wide frame acceptable?

YES NO **Wide Shot test:** Any problematicvisual elements in the frame?

YES NO **360 test:** Are there any problematic directions that should be avoided?

YES NO **Commercial clearance:** Any properties that require commercial clearance?

YES NO **Indoor staging:** Does the crew, cast and gear fit inside?

YES NO **VFX Need:** Would anything need to be removed or added in post?

YES NO **Indoor staging:** Any special production design needs?

YES NO **Sunlight:** Any sunlight consideration?

○ morning   ○ noon   ○ afternoon   ○ evening   ○ night

Notes:

SOUND

YES NO **HVAC:** Can you turn off the heating, ventilation and air conditioning unit?

YES NO **Refrigerators:** Can you turn off any noisy ? appliances or refrigerators?

YES NO **Reverberation:** Can you record clean dialog?

YES NO **Reverberation:** Do you need to dampen echoes in the space?

Notes:

👤 SURROUNDINGS

[YES] [NO] **Roads & Traffic:** Noise or continuity issues from vehicles or pedestrians?

[YES] [NO] **Schools:** Noise or other issues connected with students?

[YES] [NO] **Playgrounds:** Will noise affected the sound or will people be in the frame?

[YES] [NO] **Factories:** Any noise generated from the machines or any road issues?

[YES] [NO] **Gas station:** Any noise or traffic issues?

[YES] [NO] **Parking:** Is there sufficient parking for talent, crew, and production vehicles?

[YES] [NO] **Airports:** Noise or activity and traffic issues and concerns?

[YES] [NO] **Air traffic:** Any significant air traffic overhead and sound concerns?

[YES] [NO] **Subway:** Will subway noise fit to the scene? Will it affect sound recording?

[YES] [NO] **Subway:** Will subway noise fit to the scene? Will it affect sound recording?

[YES] [NO] **Train station:** Will train noise fit in the scene? Any train appear in the frame?

[YES] [NO] **Staging Talent:** Is there a quiet place dedicated for talent, extras, crew?

[YES] [NO] **Restrooms:** Is there a enough restrooms for all?

Notes:

☂ WEATHER

[YES] [NO] **Temperature:** Is there temperature control?

[YES] [NO] **Rain / snow:** Will precipitation have a potential impact on the shoot?

[YES] [NO] **Indoor:** Will sound from precipitation have a potential impact on the shoot?

Notes:

🔌 POWER

[ ] How many accessible outlets?

[YES] [NO] **Access:** Does the electrical crew has access to the circuit breaker box?

[YES] [NO] **Hair and makeup:** Is there a dedicated space and breaker for Hair & Makeup?

🚰 FACILITIES

[ ] How many people on set to every available bathroom?

[YES] [NO] Access to **Water Shut Off** in case of emergency

[YES] [NO] Access to **Gas Shut Off** in case of emergency

Notes:

🤝 CONTRACTS

[YES] [NO] **Contract:** Has the location owner sign the contract/location release?

[YES] [NO] **Insurance:** Does the production insurance cover the location?

Dates needed: Total number of days: Total cost:

Contact person:

Phone: email:

LOCATION SCOUTING CHECKLIST

Project:

Director:

Producer:

Location scout:

Scene: Scene Number:

Location name:

Address:

STORY

☐ **Storytelling:** Does the location meet the scene requirements and fit the director's tone?

☐ **Anachronism:** Does the setting fit the time period and story setting?

Notes:

SIGHT

○ interior   ○ exterior

[YES] [NO] **Wide Shot test:** Wide frame acceptable?

[YES] [NO] **Wide Shot test:** Any problematicvisual elements in the frame?

[YES] [NO] **360 test:** Are there any problematic directions that should be avoided?

[YES] [NO] **Commercial clearance:** Any properties that require commercial clearance?

[YES] [NO] **Indoor staging:** Does the crew, cast and gear fit inside?

[YES] [NO] **VFX Need:** Would anything need to be removed or added in post?

[YES] [NO] **Indoor staging:** Any special production design needs?

[YES] [NO] **Sunlight:** Any sunlight consideration?

○ morning   ○ noon   ○ afternoon   ○ evening   ○ night

Notes:

SOUND

[YES] [NO] **HVAC:** Can you turn off the heating, ventilation and air conditioning unit?

[YES] [NO] **Refrigerators:** Can you turn off any noisy ? appliances or refrigerators?

[YES] [NO] **Reverberation:** Can you record clean dialog?

[YES] [NO] **Reverberation:** Do you need to dampen echoes in the space?

Notes:

LOCATION SCOUTING CHECKLIST

SURROUNDINGS

[YES] [NO] **Roads & Traffic:** Noise or continuity issues from vehicles or pedestrians?

[YES] [NO] **Schools:** Noise or other issues connected with students?

[YES] [NO] **Playgrounds:** Will noise affected the sound or will people be in the frame?

[YES] [NO] **Factories:** Any noise generated from the machines or any road issues?

[YES] [NO] **Gas station:** Any noise or traffic issues?

[YES] [NO] **Parking:** Is there sufficient parking for talent, crew, and production vehicles?

[YES] [NO] **Airports:** Noise or activity and traffic issues and concerns?

[YES] [NO] **Air traffic:** Any significant air traffic overhead and sound concerns?

[YES] [NO] **Subway:** Will subway noise fit to the scene? Will it affect sound recording?

[YES] [NO] **Subway:** Will subway noise fit to the scene? Will it affect sound recording?

[YES] [NO] **Train station:** Will train noise fit in the scene? Any train appear in the frame?

[YES] [NO] **Staging Talent:** Is there a quiet place dedicated for talent, extras, crew?

[YES] [NO] **Restrooms:** Is there a enough restrooms for all?

Notes:

WEATHER

[YES] [NO] **Temperature:** Is there temperature control?

[YES] [NO] **Rain / snow:** Will precipitation have a potential impact on the shoot?

[YES] [NO] **Indoor:** Will sound from precipitation have a potential impact on the shoot?

Notes:

POWER

[ ] How many accessible outlets?

[YES] [NO] **Access:** Does the electrical crew has access to the circuit breaker box?

[YES] [NO] **Hair and makeup:** Is there a dedicated space and breaker for Hair & Makeup?

FACILITIES

[ ] How many people on set to every available bathroom?

[YES] [NO] Access to **Water Shut Off** in case of emergency

[YES] [NO] Access to **Gas Shut Off** in case of emergency

Notes:

CONTRACTS

[YES] [NO] **Contract:** Has the location owner sign the contract/location release?

[YES] [NO] **Insurance:** Does the production insurance cover the location?

Dates needed: _____ Total number of days: _____ Total cost: _____

Contact person: _____

Phone: _____ email: _____

LOCATION SCOUTING CHECKLIST

Project:

Director:

Producer:

Location scout:

Scene: Scene Number:

Location name:

Address:

STORY

☐ **Storytelling:** Does the location meet the scene requirements and fit the director's tone?

☐ **Anachronism:** Does the setting fit the time period and story setting?

Notes:

SIGHT

◯ interior   ◯ exterior

[YES] [NO] **Wide Shot test:** Wide frame acceptable?

[YES] [NO] **Wide Shot test:** Any problematicvisual elements in the frame?

[YES] [NO] **360 test:** Are there any problematic directions that should be avoided?

[YES] [NO] **Commercial clearance:** Any properties that require commercial clearance?

[YES] [NO] **Indoor staging:** Does the crew, cast and gear fit inside?

[YES] [NO] **VFX Need:** Would anything need to be removed or added in post?

[YES] [NO] **Indoor staging:** Any special production design needs?

[YES] [NO] **Sunlight:** Any sunlight consideration?

◯ morning   ◯ noon   ◯ afternoon   ◯ evening   ◯ night

Notes:

SOUND

[YES] [NO] **HVAC:** Can you turn off the heating, ventilation and air conditioning unit?

[YES] [NO] **Refrigerators:** Can you turn off any noisy ? appliances or refrigerators?

[YES] [NO] **Reverberation:** Can you record clean dialog?

[YES] [NO] **Reverberation:** Do you need to dampen echoes in the space?

Notes:

SURROUNDINGS

YES	NO	**Roads & Traffic:** Noise or continuity issues from vehicles or pedestrians?
YES	NO	**Schools:** Noise or other issues connected with students?
YES	NO	**Playgrounds:** Will noise affected the sound or will people be in the frame?
YES	NO	**Factories:** Any noise generated from the machines or any road issues?
YES	NO	**Gas station:** Any noise or traffic issues?
YES	NO	**Parking:** Is there sufficient parking for talent, crew, and production vehicles?

YES	NO	**Airports:** Noise or activity and traffic issues and concerns?
YES	NO	**Air traffic:** Any significant air traffic overhead and sound concerns?
YES	NO	**Subway:** Will subway noise fit to the scene? Will it affect sound recording?
YES	NO	**Subway:** Will subway noise fit to the scene? Will it affect sound recording?
YES	NO	**Train station:** Will train noise fit in the scene? Any train appear in the frame?
YES	NO	**Staging Talent:** Is there a quiet place dedicated for talent, extras, crew?
YES	NO	**Restrooms:** Is there a enough restrooms for all?

Notes:

WEATHER

| YES | NO | **Temperature:** Is there temperature control? |

| YES | NO | **Rain / snow:** Will precipitation have a potential impact on the shoot? |
| YES | NO | **Indoor:** Will sound from precipitation have a potential impact on the shoot? |

Notes:

POWER

☐ How many accessible outlets?

| YES | NO | **Access:** Does the electrical crew has access to the circuit breaker box? |
| YES | NO | **Hair and makeup:** Is there a dedicated space and breaker for Hair & Makeup? |

FACILITIES

☐ How many people on set to every available bathroom?

| YES | NO | Access to **Water Shut Off** in case of emergency |
| YES | NO | Access to **Gas Shut Off** in case of emergency |

Notes:

CONTRACTS

| YES | NO | **Contract:** Has the location owner sign the contract/location release? |

| YES | NO | **Insurance:** Does the production insurance cover the location? |

Dates needed: Total number of days: Total cost:

Contact person:

Phone: email:

LOCATION SCOUTING CHECKLIST

Project:

Director:

Producer:

Location scout:

Scene: Scene Number:

Location name:

Address:

STORY

☐ **Storytelling:** Does the location meet the scene requirements and fit the director's tone?

☐ **Anachronism:** Does the setting fit the time period and story setting?

Notes:

SIGHT

○ interior   ○ exterior

YES **NO** **Wide Shot test:** Wide frame acceptable?

YES **NO** **Wide Shot test:** Any problematic visual elements in the frame?

YES **NO** **360 test:** Are there any problematic directions that should be avoided?

YES **NO** **Commercial clearance:** Any properties that require commercial clearance?

YES **NO** **Indoor staging:** Does the crew, cast and gear fit inside?

YES **NO** **VFX Need:** Would anything need to be removed or added in post?

YES **NO** **Indoor staging:** Any special production design needs?

YES **NO** **Sunlight:** Any sunlight consideration?

○ morning ○ noon ○ afternoon ○ evening ○ night

Notes:

SOUND

YES **NO** **HVAC:** Can you turn off the heating, ventilation and air conditioning unit?

YES **NO** **Refrigerators:** Can you turn off any noisy? appliances or refrigerators?

YES **NO** **Reverberation:** Can you record clean dialog?

YES **NO** **Reverberation:** Do you need to dampen echoes in the space?

Notes:

LOCATION SCOUTING CHECKLIST

SURROUNDINGS

[YES] [NO] **Roads & Traffic:** Noise or continuity issues from vehicles or pedestrians?

[YES] [NO] **Schools:** Noise or other issues connected with students?

[YES] [NO] **Playgrounds:** Will noise affected the sound or will people be in the frame?

[YES] [NO] **Factories:** Any noise generated from the machines or any road issues?

[YES] [NO] **Gas station:** Any noise or traffic issues?

[YES] [NO] **Parking:** Is there sufficient parking for talent, crew, and production vehicles?

[YES] [NO] **Airports:** Noise or activity and traffic issues and concerns?

[YES] [NO] **Air traffic:** Any significant air traffic overhead and sound concerns?

[YES] [NO] **Subway:** Will subway noise fit to the scene? Will it affect sound recording?

[YES] [NO] **Subway:** Will subway noise fit to the scene? Will it affect sound recording?

[YES] [NO] **Train station:** Will train noise fit in the scene? Any train appear in the frame?

[YES] [NO] **Staging Talent:** Is there a quiet place dedicated for talent, extras, crew?

[YES] [NO] **Restrooms:** Is there a enough restrooms for all?

Notes:

WEATHER

[YES] [NO] **Temperature:** Is there temperature control?

[YES] [NO] **Rain / snow:** Will precipitation have a potential impact on the shoot?

[YES] [NO] **Indoor:** Will sound from precipitation have a potential impact on the shoot?

Notes:

POWER

[ ] How many accessible outlets?

[YES] [NO] **Access:** Does the electrical crew has access to the circuit breaker box?

[YES] [NO] **Hair and makeup:** Is there a dedicated space and breaker for Hair & Makeup?

FACILITIES

[ ] How many people on set to every available bathroom?

[YES] [NO] Access to **Water Shut Off** in case of emergency

[YES] [NO] Access to **Gas Shut Off** in case of emergency

Notes:

CONTRACTS

[YES] [NO] **Contract:** Has the location owner sign the contract/location release?

[YES] [NO] **Insurance:** Does the production insurance cover the location?

Dates needed: _____ Total number of days: _____ Total cost: _____

Contact person: _____

Phone: _____ email: _____

LOCATION SCOUTING CHECKLIST

Project:

Director:

Producer:

Location scout:

Scene: Scene Number:

Location name:

Address:

STORY

☐ **Storytelling:** Does the location meet the scene requirements and fit the director's tone?

☐ **Anachronism:** Does the setting fit the time period and story setting?

Notes:

SIGHT

○ interior ○ exterior

☐ YES ☐ NO **Wide Shot test:** Wide frame acceptable?

☐ YES ☐ NO **Wide Shot test:** Any problematic visual elements in the frame?

☐ YES ☐ NO **360 test:** Are there any problematic directions that should be avoided?

☐ YES ☐ NO **Commercial clearance:** Any properties that require commercial clearance?

☐ YES ☐ NO **Indoor staging:** Does the crew, cast and gear fit inside?

☐ YES ☐ NO **VFX Need:** Would anything need to be removed or added in post?

☐ YES ☐ NO **Indoor staging:** Any special production design needs?

☐ YES ☐ NO **Sunlight:** Any sunlight consideration?

○ morning ○ noon ○ afternoon ○ evening ○ night

Notes:

SOUND

☐ YES ☐ NO **HVAC:** Can you turn off the heating, ventilation and air conditioning unit?

☐ YES ☐ NO **Refrigerators:** Can you turn off any noisy ? appliances or refrigerators?

☐ YES ☐ NO **Reverberation:** Can you record clean dialog?

☐ YES ☐ NO **Reverberation:** Do you need to dampen echoes in the space?

Notes:

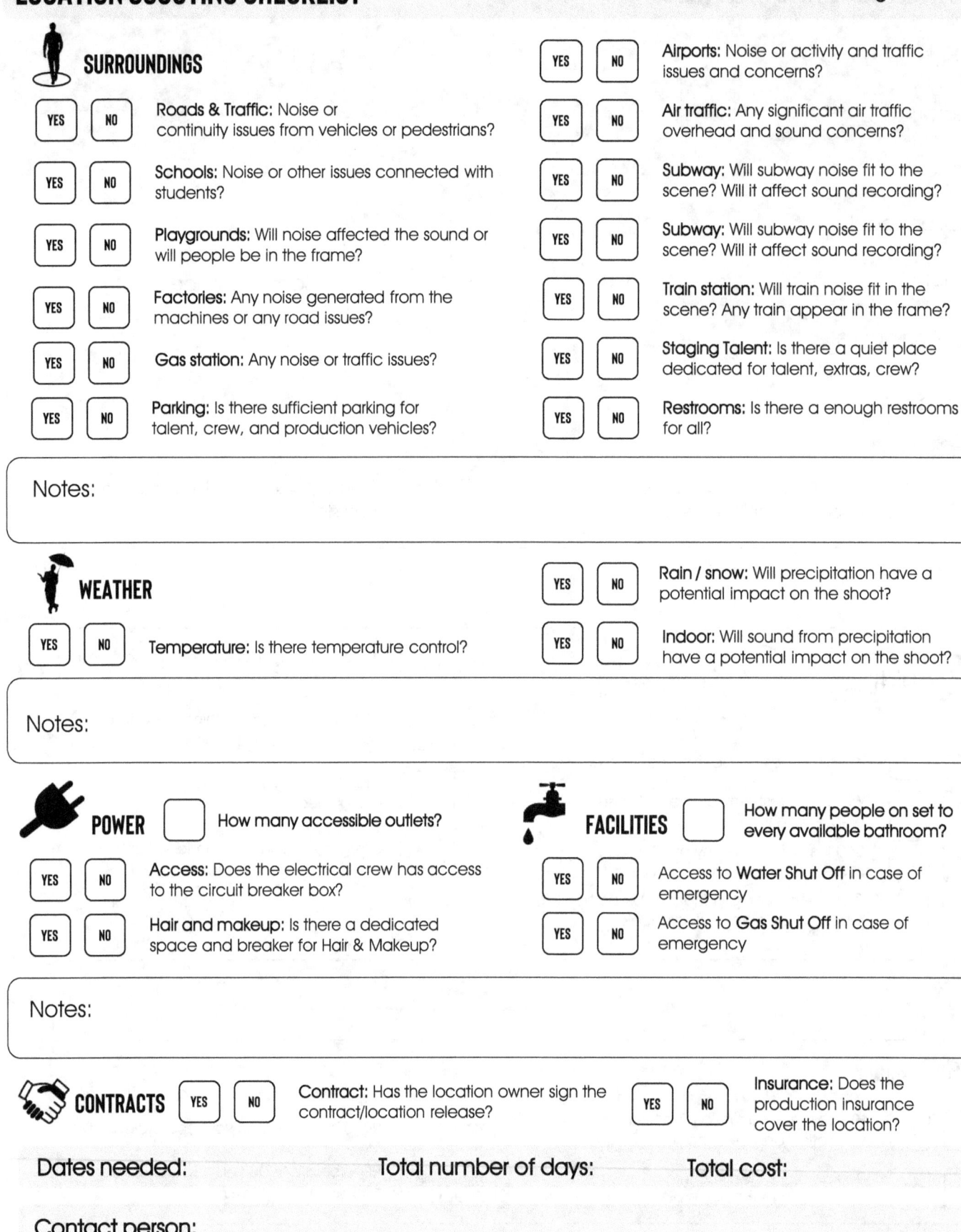

SURROUNDINGS

[YES] [NO] **Roads & Traffic:** Noise or continuity issues from vehicles or pedestrians?

[YES] [NO] **Schools:** Noise or other issues connected with students?

[YES] [NO] **Playgrounds:** Will noise affected the sound or will people be in the frame?

[YES] [NO] **Factories:** Any noise generated from the machines or any road issues?

[YES] [NO] **Gas station:** Any noise or traffic issues?

[YES] [NO] **Parking:** Is there sufficient parking for talent, crew, and production vehicles?

[YES] [NO] **Airports:** Noise or activity and traffic issues and concerns?

[YES] [NO] **Air traffic:** Any significant air traffic overhead and sound concerns?

[YES] [NO] **Subway:** Will subway noise fit to the scene? Will it affect sound recording?

[YES] [NO] **Subway:** Will subway noise fit to the scene? Will it affect sound recording?

[YES] [NO] **Train station:** Will train noise fit in the scene? Any train appear in the frame?

[YES] [NO] **Staging Talent:** Is there a quiet place dedicated for talent, extras, crew?

[YES] [NO] **Restrooms:** Is there a enough restrooms for all?

Notes:

WEATHER

[YES] [NO] **Temperature:** Is there temperature control?

[YES] [NO] **Rain / snow:** Will precipitation have a potential impact on the shoot?

[YES] [NO] **Indoor:** Will sound from precipitation have a potential impact on the shoot?

Notes:

POWER [ ] How many accessible outlets?

[YES] [NO] **Access:** Does the electrical crew has access to the circuit breaker box?

[YES] [NO] **Hair and makeup:** Is there a dedicated space and breaker for Hair & Makeup?

FACILITIES [ ] How many people on set to every available bathroom?

[YES] [NO] Access to **Water Shut Off** in case of emergency

[YES] [NO] Access to **Gas Shut Off** in case of emergency

Notes:

CONTRACTS [YES] [NO] **Contract:** Has the location owner sign the contract/location release?

[YES] [NO] **Insurance:** Does the production insurance cover the location?

Dates needed: _____ Total number of days: _____ Total cost: _____

Contact person: _____

Phone: _____ email: _____

LOCATION SCOUTING CHECKLIST

Project:

Director:

Producer:

Location scout:

Scene: Scene Number:

Location name:

Address:

STORY

☐ **Storytelling:** Does the location meet the scene requirements and fit the director's tone?

☐ **Anachronism:** Does the setting fit the time period and story setting?

Notes:

SIGHT

○ interior   ○ exterior

[YES] [NO] **Wide Shot test:** Wide frame acceptable?

[YES] [NO] **Wide Shot test:** Any problematicvisual elements in the frame?

[YES] [NO] **360 test:** Are there any problematic directions that should be avoided?

[YES] [NO] **Commercial clearance:** Any properties that require commercial clearance?

[YES] [NO] **Indoor staging:** Does the crew, cast and gear fit inside?

[YES] [NO] **VFX Need:** Would anything need to be removed or added in post?

[YES] [NO] **Indoor staging:** Any special production design needs?

[YES] [NO] **Sunlight:** Any sunlight consideration?

○ morning   ○ noon   ○ afternoon   ○ evening   ○ night

Notes:

SOUND

[YES] [NO] **HVAC:** Can you turn off the heating, ventilation and air conditioning unit?

[YES] [NO] **Refrigerators:** Can you turn off any noisy ? appliances or refrigerators?

[YES] [NO] **Reverberation:** Can you record clean dialog?

[YES] [NO] **Reverberation:** Do you need to dampen echoes in the space?

Notes:

LOCATION SCOUTING CHECKLIST

SURROUNDINGS

- [ ] YES [ ] NO **Roads & Traffic:** Noise or continuity issues from vehicles or pedestrians?
- [ ] YES [ ] NO **Schools:** Noise or other issues connected with students?
- [ ] YES [ ] NO **Playgrounds:** Will noise affected the sound or will people be in the frame?
- [ ] YES [ ] NO **Factories:** Any noise generated from the machines or any road issues?
- [ ] YES [ ] NO **Gas station:** Any noise or traffic issues?
- [ ] YES [ ] NO **Parking:** Is there sufficient parking for talent, crew, and production vehicles?

- [ ] YES [ ] NO **Airports:** Noise or activity and traffic issues and concerns?
- [ ] YES [ ] NO **Air traffic:** Any significant air traffic overhead and sound concerns?
- [ ] YES [ ] NO **Subway:** Will subway noise fit to the scene? Will it affect sound recording?
- [ ] YES [ ] NO **Subway:** Will subway noise fit to the scene? Will it affect sound recording?
- [ ] YES [ ] NO **Train station:** Will train noise fit in the scene? Any train appear in the frame?
- [ ] YES [ ] NO **Staging Talent:** Is there a quiet place dedicated for talent, extras, crew?
- [ ] YES [ ] NO **Restrooms:** Is there a enough restrooms for all?

Notes:

WEATHER

- [ ] YES [ ] NO **Temperature:** Is there temperature control?

- [ ] YES [ ] NO **Rain / snow:** Will precipitation have a potential impact on the shoot?
- [ ] YES [ ] NO **Indoor:** Will sound from precipitation have a potential impact on the shoot?

Notes:

POWER [ ] How many accessible outlets?

- [ ] YES [ ] NO **Access:** Does the electrical crew has access to the circuit breaker box?
- [ ] YES [ ] NO **Hair and makeup:** Is there a dedicated space and breaker for Hair & Makeup?

FACILITIES [ ] How many people on set to every available bathroom?

- [ ] YES [ ] NO Access to **Water Shut Off** in case of emergency
- [ ] YES [ ] NO Access to **Gas Shut Off** in case of emergency

Notes:

CONTRACTS

[ ] YES [ ] NO **Contract:** Has the location owner sign the contract/location release?

[ ] YES [ ] NO **Insurance:** Does the production insurance cover the location?

Dates needed: Total number of days: Total cost:

Contact person:

Phone: email:

LOCATION SCOUTING CHECKLIST

Project:

Director:

Producer:

Location scout:

Scene: Scene Number:

Location name:

Address:

STORY

☐ **Storytelling:** Does the location meet the scene requirements and fit the director's tone?

☐ **Anachronism:** Does the setting fit the time period and story setting?

Notes:

SIGHT

○ interior   ○ exterior

[YES] [NO] **Wide Shot test:** Wide frame acceptable?

[YES] [NO] **Wide Shot test:** Any problematicvisual elements in the frame?

[YES] [NO] **360 test:** Are there any problematic directions that should be avoided?

[YES] [NO] **Commercial clearance:** Any properties that require commercial clearance?

[YES] [NO] **Indoor staging:** Does the crew, cast and gear fit inside?

[YES] [NO] **VFX Need:** Would anything need to be removed or added in post?

[YES] [NO] **Indoor staging:** Any special production design needs?

[YES] [NO] **Sunlight:** Any sunlight consideration?

○ morning   ○ noon   ○ afternoon   ○ evening   ○ night

Notes:

SOUND

[YES] [NO] **HVAC:** Can you turn off the heating, ventilation and air conditioning unit?

[YES] [NO] **Refrigerators:** Can you turn off any noisy ? appliances or refrigerators?

[YES] [NO] **Reverberation:** Can you record clean dialog?

[YES] [NO] **Reverberation:** Do you need to dampen echoes in the space?

Notes:

SURROUNDINGS

[YES] [NO] **Roads & Traffic:** Noise or continuity issues from vehicles or pedestrians?

[YES] [NO] **Schools:** Noise or other issues connected with students?

[YES] [NO] **Playgrounds:** Will noise affected the sound or will people be in the frame?

[YES] [NO] **Factories:** Any noise generated from the machines or any road issues?

[YES] [NO] **Gas station:** Any noise or traffic issues?

[YES] [NO] **Parking:** Is there sufficient parking for talent, crew, and production vehicles?

[YES] [NO] **Airports:** Noise or activity and traffic issues and concerns?

[YES] [NO] **Air traffic:** Any significant air traffic overhead and sound concerns?

[YES] [NO] **Subway:** Will subway noise fit to the scene? Will it affect sound recording?

[YES] [NO] **Subway:** Will subway noise fit to the scene? Will it affect sound recording?

[YES] [NO] **Train station:** Will train noise fit in the scene? Any train appear in the frame?

[YES] [NO] **Staging Talent:** Is there a quiet place dedicated for talent, extras, crew?

[YES] [NO] **Restrooms:** Is there a enough restrooms for all?

Notes:

WEATHER

[YES] [NO] **Temperature:** Is there temperature control?

[YES] [NO] **Rain / snow:** Will precipitation have a potential impact on the shoot?

[YES] [NO] **Indoor:** Will sound from precipitation have a potential impact on the shoot?

Notes:

POWER

[ ] How many accessible outlets?

[YES] [NO] **Access:** Does the electrical crew has access to the circuit breaker box?

[YES] [NO] **Hair and makeup:** Is there a dedicated space and breaker for Hair & Makeup?

FACILITIES

[ ] How many people on set to every available bathroom?

[YES] [NO] Access to **Water Shut Off** in case of emergency

[YES] [NO] Access to **Gas Shut Off** in case of emergency

Notes:

CONTRACTS

[YES] [NO] **Contract:** Has the location owner sign the contract/location release?

[YES] [NO] **Insurance:** Does the production insurance cover the location?

Dates needed: _____ Total number of days: _____ Total cost: _____

Contact person: _____

Phone: _____   email: _____

LOCATION SCOUTING CHECKLIST

Project:

Director:

Producer:

Location scout:

Scene: Scene Number:

Location name:

Address:

STORY

☐ **Storytelling:** Does the location meet the scene requirements and fit the director's tone?

☐ **Anachronism:** Does the setting fit the time period and story setting?

Notes:

SIGHT

○ interior   ○ exterior

YES	NO	**Wide Shot test:** Wide frame acceptable?
YES	NO	**Wide Shot test:** Any problematicvisual elements in the frame?
YES	NO	**360 test:** Are there any problematic directions that should be avoided?
YES	NO	**Commercial clearance:** Any properties that require commercial clearance?

YES	NO	**Indoor staging:** Does the crew, cast and gear fit inside?
YES	NO	**VFX Need:** Would anything need to be removed or added in post?
YES	NO	**Indoor staging:** Any special production design needs?
YES	NO	**Sunlight:** Any sunlight consideration?

○ morning   ○ noon   ○ afternoon   ○ evening   ○ night

Notes:

SOUND

| YES | NO | **HVAC:** Can you turn off the heating, ventilation and air conditioning unit? |
| YES | NO | **Refrigerators:** Can you turn off any noisy ? appliances or refrigerators? |

| YES | NO | **Reverberation:** Can you record clean dialog? |
| YES | NO | **Reverberation:** Do you need to dampen echoes in the space? |

Notes:

LOCATION SCOUTING CHECKLIST

SURROUNDINGS

[YES] [NO] **Roads & Traffic:** Noise or continuity issues from vehicles or pedestrians?

[YES] [NO] **Schools:** Noise or other issues connected with students?

[YES] [NO] **Playgrounds:** Will noise affected the sound or will people be in the frame?

[YES] [NO] **Factories:** Any noise generated from the machines or any road issues?

[YES] [NO] **Gas station:** Any noise or traffic issues?

[YES] [NO] **Parking:** Is there sufficient parking for talent, crew, and production vehicles?

[YES] [NO] **Airports:** Noise or activity and traffic issues and concerns?

[YES] [NO] **Air traffic:** Any significant air traffic overhead and sound concerns?

[YES] [NO] **Subway:** Will subway noise fit to the scene? Will it affect sound recording?

[YES] [NO] **Subway:** Will subway noise fit to the scene? Will it affect sound recording?

[YES] [NO] **Train station:** Will train noise fit in the scene? Any train appear in the frame?

[YES] [NO] **Staging Talent:** Is there a quiet place dedicated for talent, extras, crew?

[YES] [NO] **Restrooms:** Is there a enough restrooms for all?

Notes:

WEATHER

[YES] [NO] **Temperature:** Is there temperature control?

[YES] [NO] **Rain / snow:** Will precipitation have a potential impact on the shoot?

[YES] [NO] **Indoor:** Will sound from precipitation have a potential impact on the shoot?

Notes:

POWER

[   ] How many accessible outlets?

[YES] [NO] **Access:** Does the electrical crew has access to the circuit breaker box?

[YES] [NO] **Hair and makeup:** Is there a dedicated space and breaker for Hair & Makeup?

FACILITIES

[   ] How many people on set to every available bathroom?

[YES] [NO] Access to **Water Shut Off** in case of emergency

[YES] [NO] Access to **Gas Shut Off** in case of emergency

Notes:

CONTRACTS

[YES] [NO] **Contract:** Has the location owner sign the contract/location release?

[YES] [NO] **Insurance:** Does the production insurance cover the location?

Dates needed: Total number of days: Total cost:

Contact person:

Phone: email:

LOCATION SCOUTING CHECKLIST

Project:

Director:

Producer:

Location scout:

Scene: Scene Number:

Location name:

Address:

STORY

☐ **Storytelling:** Does the location meet the scene requirements and fit the director's tone?

☐ **Anachronism:** Does the setting fit the time period and story setting?

Notes:

SIGHT

◯ interior   ◯ exterior

[YES] [NO] **Wide Shot test:** Wide frame acceptable?

[YES] [NO] **Wide Shot test:** Any problematic visual elements in the frame?

[YES] [NO] **360 test:** Are there any problematic directions that should be avoided?

[YES] [NO] **Commercial clearance:** Any properties that require commercial clearance?

[YES] [NO] **Indoor staging:** Does the crew, cast and gear fit inside?

[YES] [NO] **VFX Need:** Would anything need to be removed or added in post?

[YES] [NO] **Indoor staging:** Any special production design needs?

[YES] [NO] **Sunlight:** Any sunlight consideration?

◯ morning   ◯ noon   ◯ afternoon   ◯ evening   ◯ night

Notes:

SOUND

[YES] [NO] **HVAC:** Can you turn off the heating, ventilation and air conditioning unit?

[YES] [NO] **Refrigerators:** Can you turn off any noisy ? appliances or refrigerators?

[YES] [NO] **Reverberation:** Can you record clean dialog?

[YES] [NO] **Reverberation:** Do you need to dampen echoes in the space?

Notes:

SURROUNDINGS

[YES] [NO] **Roads & Traffic:** Noise or continuity issues from vehicles or pedestrians?

[YES] [NO] **Schools:** Noise or other issues connected with students?

[YES] [NO] **Playgrounds:** Will noise affected the sound or will people be in the frame?

[YES] [NO] **Factories:** Any noise generated from the machines or any road issues?

[YES] [NO] **Gas station:** Any noise or traffic issues?

[YES] [NO] **Parking:** Is there sufficient parking for talent, crew, and production vehicles?

[YES] [NO] **Airports:** Noise or activity and traffic issues and concerns?

[YES] [NO] **Air traffic:** Any significant air traffic overhead and sound concerns?

[YES] [NO] **Subway:** Will subway noise fit to the scene? Will it affect sound recording?

[YES] [NO] **Subway:** Will subway noise fit to the scene? Will it affect sound recording?

[YES] [NO] **Train station:** Will train noise fit in the scene? Any train appear in the frame?

[YES] [NO] **Staging Talent:** Is there a quiet place dedicated for talent, extras, crew?

[YES] [NO] **Restrooms:** Is there a enough restrooms for all?

Notes:

WEATHER

[YES] [NO] **Temperature:** Is there temperature control?

[YES] [NO] **Rain / snow:** Will precipitation have a potential impact on the shoot?

[YES] [NO] **Indoor:** Will sound from precipitation have a potential impact on the shoot?

Notes:

POWER

[ ] How many accessible outlets?

[YES] [NO] **Access:** Does the electrical crew has access to the circuit breaker box?

[YES] [NO] **Hair and makeup:** Is there a dedicated space and breaker for Hair & Makeup?

FACILITIES

[ ] How many people on set to every available bathroom?

[YES] [NO] Access to **Water Shut Off** in case of emergency

[YES] [NO] Access to **Gas Shut Off** in case of emergency

Notes:

CONTRACTS

[YES] [NO] **Contract:** Has the location owner sign the contract/location release?

[YES] [NO] **Insurance:** Does the production insurance cover the location?

Dates needed: Total number of days: Total cost:

Contact person:

Phone: email:

LOCATION SCOUTING CHECKLIST

Project:

Director:

Producer:

Location scout:

Scene: Scene Number:

Location name:

Address:

STORY

☐ **Storytelling:** Does the location meet the scene requirements and fit the director's tone?

☐ **Anachronism:** Does the setting fit the time period and story setting?

Notes:

SIGHT

◯ interior   ◯ exterior

YES | NO   **Wide Shot test:** Wide frame acceptable?

YES | NO   **Wide Shot test:** Any problematic visual elements in the frame?

YES | NO   **360 test:** Are there any problematic directions that should be avoided?

YES | NO   **Commercial clearance:** Any properties that require commercial clearance?

YES | NO   **Indoor staging:** Does the crew, cast and gear fit inside?

YES | NO   **VFX Need:** Would anything need to be removed or added in post?

YES | NO   **Indoor staging:** Any special production design needs?

YES | NO   **Sunlight:** Any sunlight consideration?

◯ morning   ◯ noon   ◯ afternoon   ◯ evening   ◯ night

Notes:

SOUND

YES | NO   **HVAC:** Can you turn off the heating, ventilation and air conditioning unit?

YES | NO   **Refrigerators:** Can you turn off any noisy ? appliances or refrigerators?

YES | NO   **Reverberation:** Can you record clean dialog?

YES | NO   **Reverberation:** Do you need to dampen echoes in the space?

Notes:

LOCATION SCOUTING CHECKLIST

SURROUNDINGS

YES	NO	**Roads & Traffic:** Noise or continuity issues from vehicles or pedestrians?
YES	NO	**Schools:** Noise or other issues connected with students?
YES	NO	**Playgrounds:** Will noise affected the sound or will people be in the frame?
YES	NO	**Factories:** Any noise generated from the machines or any road issues?
YES	NO	**Gas station:** Any noise or traffic issues?
YES	NO	**Parking:** Is there sufficient parking for talent, crew, and production vehicles?

YES	NO	**Airports:** Noise or activity and traffic issues and concerns?
YES	NO	**Air traffic:** Any significant air traffic overhead and sound concerns?
YES	NO	**Subway:** Will subway noise fit to the scene? Will it affect sound recording?
YES	NO	**Subway:** Will subway noise fit to the scene? Will it affect sound recording?
YES	NO	**Train station:** Will train noise fit in the scene? Any train appear in the frame?
YES	NO	**Staging Talent:** Is there a quiet place dedicated for talent, extras, crew?
YES	NO	**Restrooms:** Is there a enough restrooms for all?

Notes:

WEATHER

| YES | NO | **Temperature:** Is there temperature control? |

| YES | NO | **Rain / snow:** Will precipitation have a potential impact on the shoot? |
| YES | NO | **Indoor:** Will sound from precipitation have a potential impact on the shoot? |

Notes:

POWER

[ ] How many accessible outlets?

| YES | NO | **Access:** Does the electrical crew has access to the circuit breaker box? |
| YES | NO | **Hair and makeup:** Is there a dedicated space and breaker for Hair & Makeup? |

FACILITIES

[ ] How many people on set to every available bathroom?

| YES | NO | Access to **Water Shut Off** in case of emergency |
| YES | NO | Access to **Gas Shut Off** in case of emergency |

Notes:

CONTRACTS

| YES | NO | **Contract:** Has the location owner sign the contract/location release? |
| YES | NO | **Insurance:** Does the production insurance cover the location? |

Dates needed: _____ Total number of days: _____ Total cost: _____

Contact person: _____

Phone: _____ email: _____

LOCATION SCOUTING CHECKLIST

Project:

Director:

Producer:

Location scout:

Scene: Scene Number:

Location name:

Address:

STORY

☐ **Storytelling:** Does the location meet the scene requirements and fit the director's tone?

☐ **Anachronism:** Does the setting fit the time period and story setting?

Notes:

SIGHT

○ interior   ○ exterior

YES NO **Wide Shot test:** Wide frame acceptable?

YES NO **Wide Shot test:** Any problematicvisual elements in the frame?

YES NO **360 test:** Are there any problematic directions that should be avoided?

YES NO **Commercial clearance:** Any properties that require commercial clearance?

YES NO **Indoor staging:** Does the crew, cast and gear fit inside?

YES NO **VFX Need:** Would anything need to be removed or added in post?

YES NO **Indoor staging:** Any special production design needs?

YES NO **Sunlight:** Any sunlight consideration?

○ morning   ○ noon   ○ afternoon   ○ evening   ○ night

Notes:

SOUND

YES NO **HVAC:** Can you turn off the heating, ventilation and air conditioning unit?

YES NO **Refrigerators:** Can you turn off any noisy ? appliances or refrigerators?

YES NO **Reverberation:** Can you record clean dialog?

YES NO **Reverberation:** Do you need to dampen echoes in the space?

Notes:

LOCATION SCOUTING CHECKLIST

SURROUNDINGS

YES / NO	**Roads & Traffic:** Noise or continuity issues from vehicles or pedestrians?	
YES / NO	**Schools:** Noise or other issues connected with students?	
YES / NO	**Playgrounds:** Will noise affected the sound or will people be in the frame?	
YES / NO	**Factories:** Any noise generated from the machines or any road issues?	
YES / NO	**Gas station:** Any noise or traffic issues?	
YES / NO	**Parking:** Is there sufficient parking for talent, crew, and production vehicles?	

YES / NO — **Airports:** Noise or activity and traffic issues and concerns?

YES / NO — **Air traffic:** Any significant air traffic overhead and sound concerns?

YES / NO — **Subway:** Will subway noise fit to the scene? Will it affect sound recording?

YES / NO — **Subway:** Will subway noise fit to the scene? Will it affect sound recording?

YES / NO — **Train station:** Will train noise fit in the scene? Any train appear in the frame?

YES / NO — **Staging Talent:** Is there a quiet place dedicated for talent, extras, crew?

YES / NO — **Restrooms:** Is there a enough restrooms for all?

Notes:

WEATHER

YES / NO — **Temperature:** Is there temperature control?

YES / NO — **Rain / snow:** Will precipitation have a potential impact on the shoot?

YES / NO — **Indoor:** Will sound from precipitation have a potential impact on the shoot?

Notes:

POWER

[ ] How many accessible outlets?

YES / NO — **Access:** Does the electrical crew has access to the circuit breaker box?

YES / NO — **Hair and makeup:** Is there a dedicated space and breaker for Hair & Makeup?

FACILITIES

[ ] How many people on set to every available bathroom?

YES / NO — Access to **Water Shut Off** in case of emergency

YES / NO — Access to **Gas Shut Off** in case of emergency

Notes:

CONTRACTS

YES / NO — **Contract:** Has the location owner sign the contract/location release?

YES / NO — **Insurance:** Does the production insurance cover the location?

Dates needed: _____ Total number of days: _____ Total cost: _____

Contact person: _____

Phone: _____ email: _____

LOCATION SCOUTING CHECKLIST

Project:

Director:

Producer:

Location scout:

Scene: Scene Number:

Location name:

Address:

STORY

☐ **Storytelling:** Does the location meet the scene requirements and fit the director's tone?

☐ **Anachronism:** Does the setting fit the time period and story setting?

Notes:

SIGHT

○ interior   ○ exterior

YES NO	**Wide Shot test:** Wide frame acceptable?	
YES NO	**Wide Shot test:** Any problematicvisual elements in the frame?	
YES NO	**360 test:** Are there any problematic directions that should be avoided?	
YES NO	**Commercial clearance:** Any properties that require commercial clearance?	

YES NO **Indoor staging:** Does the crew, cast and gear fit inside?

YES NO **VFX Need:** Would anything need to be removed or added in post?

YES NO **Indoor staging:** Any special production design needs?

YES NO **Sunlight:** Any sunlight consideration?

○ morning   ○ noon   ○ afternoon   ○ evening   ○ night

Notes:

SOUND

YES NO **HVAC:** Can you turn off the heating, ventilation and air conditioning unit?

YES NO **Refrigerators:** Can you turn off any noisy ? appliances or refrigerators?

YES NO **Reverberation:** Can you record clean dialog?

YES NO **Reverberation:** Do you need to dampen echoes in the space?

Notes:

SURROUNDINGS

YES / NO **Roads & Traffic:** Noise or continuity issues from vehicles or pedestrians?

YES / NO **Schools:** Noise or other issues connected with students?

YES / NO **Playgrounds:** Will noise affected the sound or will people be in the frame?

YES / NO **Factories:** Any noise generated from the machines or any road issues?

YES / NO **Gas station:** Any noise or traffic issues?

YES / NO **Parking:** Is there sufficient parking for talent, crew, and production vehicles?

YES / NO **Airports:** Noise or activity and traffic issues and concerns?

YES / NO **Air traffic:** Any significant air traffic overhead and sound concerns?

YES / NO **Subway:** Will subway noise fit to the scene? Will it affect sound recording?

YES / NO **Subway:** Will subway noise fit to the scene? Will it affect sound recording?

YES / NO **Train station:** Will train noise fit in the scene? Any train appear in the frame?

YES / NO **Staging Talent:** Is there a quiet place dedicated for talent, extras, crew?

YES / NO **Restrooms:** Is there a enough restrooms for all?

Notes:

WEATHER

YES / NO **Temperature:** Is there temperature control?

YES / NO **Rain / snow:** Will precipitation have a potential impact on the shoot?

YES / NO **Indoor:** Will sound from precipitation have a potential impact on the shoot?

Notes:

POWER

[ ] How many accessible outlets?

YES / NO **Access:** Does the electrical crew has access to the circuit breaker box?

YES / NO **Hair and makeup:** Is there a dedicated space and breaker for Hair & Makeup?

FACILITIES

[ ] How many people on set to every available bathroom?

YES / NO Access to **Water Shut Off** in case of emergency

YES / NO Access to **Gas Shut Off** in case of emergency

Notes:

CONTRACTS

YES / NO **Contract:** Has the location owner sign the contract/location release?

YES / NO **Insurance:** Does the production insurance cover the location?

Dates needed: Total number of days: Total cost:

Contact person:

Phone: email:

Project:

Director:

Producer:

Location scout:

Scene: Scene Number:

Location name:

Address:

STORY

☐ **Storytelling:** Does the location meet the scene requirements and fit the director's tone?

☐ **Anachronism:** Does the setting fit the time period and story setting?

Notes:

SIGHT

○ interior   ○ exterior

YES | NO **Wide Shot test:** Wide frame acceptable?

YES | NO **Wide Shot test:** Any problematicvisual elements in the frame?

YES | NO **360 test:** Are there any problematic directions that should be avoided?

YES | NO **Commercial clearance:** Any properties that require commercial clearance?

YES | NO **Indoor staging:** Does the crew, cast and gear fit inside?

YES | NO **VFX Need:** Would anything need to be removed or added in post?

YES | NO **Indoor staging:** Any special production design needs?

YES | NO **Sunlight:** Any sunlight consideration?

○ morning   ○ noon   ○ afternoon   ○ evening   ○ night

Notes:

SOUND

YES | NO **HVAC:** Can you turn off the heating, ventilation and air conditioning unit?

YES | NO **Refrigerators:** Can you turn off any noisy ? appliances or refrigerators?

YES | NO **Reverberation:** Can you record clean dialog?

YES | NO **Reverberation:** Do you need to dampen echoes in the space?

Notes:

SURROUNDINGS

[YES] [NO] **Roads & Traffic:** Noise or continuity issues from vehicles or pedestrians?

[YES] [NO] **Schools:** Noise or other issues connected with students?

[YES] [NO] **Playgrounds:** Will noise affected the sound or will people be in the frame?

[YES] [NO] **Factories:** Any noise generated from the machines or any road issues?

[YES] [NO] **Gas station:** Any noise or traffic issues?

[YES] [NO] **Parking:** Is there sufficient parking for talent, crew, and production vehicles?

[YES] [NO] **Airports:** Noise or activity and traffic issues and concerns?

[YES] [NO] **Air traffic:** Any significant air traffic overhead and sound concerns?

[YES] [NO] **Subway:** Will subway noise fit to the scene? Will it affect sound recording?

[YES] [NO] **Subway:** Will subway noise fit to the scene? Will it affect sound recording?

[YES] [NO] **Train station:** Will train noise fit in the scene? Any train appear in the frame?

[YES] [NO] **Staging Talent:** Is there a quiet place dedicated for talent, extras, crew?

[YES] [NO] **Restrooms:** Is there a enough restrooms for all?

Notes:

WEATHER

[YES] [NO] **Temperature:** Is there temperature control?

[YES] [NO] **Rain / snow:** Will precipitation have a potential impact on the shoot?

[YES] [NO] **Indoor:** Will sound from precipitation have a potential impact on the shoot?

Notes:

POWER

[ ] How many accessible outlets?

[YES] [NO] **Access:** Does the electrical crew has access to the circuit breaker box?

[YES] [NO] **Hair and makeup:** Is there a dedicated space and breaker for Hair & Makeup?

FACILITIES

[ ] How many people on set to every available bathroom?

[YES] [NO] Access to **Water Shut Off** in case of emergency

[YES] [NO] Access to **Gas Shut Off** in case of emergency

Notes:

CONTRACTS

[YES] [NO] **Contract:** Has the location owner sign the contract/location release?

[YES] [NO] **Insurance:** Does the production insurance cover the location?

Dates needed:

Total number of days:

Total cost:

Contact person:

Phone:

email:

Project:

Director:

Producer:

Location scout:

Scene: Scene Number:

Location name:

Address:

STORY

☐ **Storytelling:** Does the location meet the scene requirements and fit the director's tone?

☐ **Anachronism:** Does the setting fit the time period and story setting?

Notes:

SIGHT

◯ interior   ◯ exterior

YES	NO	**Indoor staging:** Does the crew, cast and gear fit inside?
YES	NO	**VFX Need:** Would anything need to be removed or added in post?
YES	NO	**Indoor staging:** Any special production design needs?
YES	NO	**Sunlight:** Any sunlight consideration?

YES	NO	**Wide Shot test:** Wide frame acceptable?
YES	NO	**Wide Shot test:** Any problematic visual elements in the frame?
YES	NO	**360 test:** Are there any problematic directions that should be avoided?
YES	NO	**Commercial clearance:** Any properties that require commercial clearance?

◯ morning ◯ noon ◯ afternoon ◯ evening ◯ night

Notes:

SOUND

YES	NO	**HVAC:** Can you turn off the heating, ventilation and air conditioning unit?
YES	NO	**Refrigerators:** Can you turn off any noisy ? appliances or refrigerators?
YES	NO	**Reverberation:** Can you record clean dialog?
YES	NO	**Reverberation:** Do you need to dampen echoes in the space?

Notes:

LOCATION SCOUTING CHECKLIST

SURROUNDINGS

[YES] [NO] Roads & Traffic: Noise or continuity issues from vehicles or pedestrians?

[YES] [NO] Schools: Noise or other issues connected with students?

[YES] [NO] Playgrounds: Will noise affected the sound or will people be in the frame?

[YES] [NO] Factories: Any noise generated from the machines or any road issues?

[YES] [NO] Gas station: Any noise or traffic issues?

[YES] [NO] Parking: Is there sufficient parking for talent, crew, and production vehicles?

[YES] [NO] Airports: Noise or activity and traffic issues and concerns?

[YES] [NO] Air traffic: Any significant air traffic overhead and sound concerns?

[YES] [NO] Subway: Will subway noise fit to the scene? Will it affect sound recording?

[YES] [NO] Subway: Will subway noise fit to the scene? Will it affect sound recording?

[YES] [NO] Train station: Will train noise fit in the scene? Any train appear in the frame?

[YES] [NO] Staging Talent: Is there a quiet place dedicated for talent, extras, crew?

[YES] [NO] Restrooms: Is there a enough restrooms for all?

Notes:

WEATHER

[YES] [NO] Temperature: Is there temperature control?

[YES] [NO] Rain / snow: Will precipitation have a potential impact on the shoot?

[YES] [NO] Indoor: Will sound from precipitation have a potential impact on the shoot?

Notes:

POWER

[ ] How many accessible outlets?

[YES] [NO] Access: Does the electrical crew has access to the circuit breaker box?

[YES] [NO] Hair and makeup: Is there a dedicated space and breaker for Hair & Makeup?

FACILITIES

[ ] How many people on set to every available bathroom?

[YES] [NO] Access to **Water Shut Off** in case of emergency

[YES] [NO] Access to **Gas Shut Off** in case of emergency

Notes:

CONTRACTS

[YES] [NO] Contract: Has the location owner sign the contract/location release?

[YES] [NO] Insurance: Does the production insurance cover the location?

Dates needed: Total number of days: Total cost:

Contact person:

Phone: email:

LOCATION SCOUTING CHECKLIST

Project:

Director:

Producer:

Location scout:

Scene: Scene Number:

Location name:

Address:

STORY

☐ **Storytelling:** Does the location meet the scene requirements and fit the director's tone?

☐ **Anachronism:** Does the setting fit the time period and story setting?

Notes:

SIGHT

○ interior   ○ exterior

☐ YES ☐ NO **Wide Shot test:** Wide frame acceptable?

☐ YES ☐ NO **Wide Shot test:** Any problematic visual elements in the frame?

☐ YES ☐ NO **360 test:** Are there any problematic directions that should be avoided?

☐ YES ☐ NO **Commercial clearance:** Any properties that require commercial clearance?

☐ YES ☐ NO **Indoor staging:** Does the crew, cast and gear fit inside?

☐ YES ☐ NO **VFX Need:** Would anything need to be removed or added in post?

☐ YES ☐ NO **Indoor staging:** Any special production design needs?

☐ YES ☐ NO **Sunlight:** Any sunlight consideration?

○ morning   ○ noon   ○ afternoon   ○ evening   ○ night

Notes:

SOUND

☐ YES ☐ NO **HVAC:** Can you turn off the heating, ventilation and air conditioning unit?

☐ YES ☐ NO **Refrigerators:** Can you turn off any noisy ? appliances or refrigerators?

☐ YES ☐ NO **Reverberation:** Can you record clean dialog?

☐ YES ☐ NO **Reverberation:** Do you need to dampen echoes in the space?

Notes:

SURROUNDINGS

[YES] [NO] Roads & Traffic: Noise or continuity issues from vehicles or pedestrians?

[YES] [NO] Schools: Noise or other issues connected with students?

[YES] [NO] Playgrounds: Will noise affected the sound or will people be in the frame?

[YES] [NO] Factories: Any noise generated from the machines or any road issues?

[YES] [NO] Gas station: Any noise or traffic issues?

[YES] [NO] Parking: Is there sufficient parking for talent, crew, and production vehicles?

[YES] [NO] Airports: Noise or activity and traffic issues and concerns?

[YES] [NO] Air traffic: Any significant air traffic overhead and sound concerns?

[YES] [NO] Subway: Will subway noise fit to the scene? Will it affect sound recording?

[YES] [NO] Subway: Will subway noise fit to the scene? Will it affect sound recording?

[YES] [NO] Train station: Will train noise fit in the scene? Any train appear in the frame?

[YES] [NO] Staging Talent: Is there a quiet place dedicated for talent, extras, crew?

[YES] [NO] Restrooms: Is there a enough restrooms for all?

Notes:

WEATHER

[YES] [NO] Temperature: Is there temperature control?

[YES] [NO] Rain / snow: Will precipitation have a potential impact on the shoot?

[YES] [NO] Indoor: Will sound from precipitation have a potential impact on the shoot?

Notes:

POWER [ ] How many accessible outlets?

[YES] [NO] Access: Does the electrical crew has access to the circuit breaker box?

[YES] [NO] Hair and makeup: Is there a dedicated space and breaker for Hair & Makeup?

FACILITIES [ ] How many people on set to every available bathroom?

[YES] [NO] Access to Water Shut Off in case of emergency

[YES] [NO] Access to Gas Shut Off in case of emergency

Notes:

CONTRACTS **[YES] [NO]** Contract: Has the location owner sign the contract/location release?

[YES] [NO] Insurance: Does the production insurance cover the location?

Dates needed: _____ Total number of days: _____ Total cost: _____

Contact person: _____

Phone: _____ email: _____

LOCATION SCOUTING CHECKLIST

Project:

Director:

Producer:

Location scout:

Scene: Scene Number:

Location name:

Address:

STORY

☐ **Storytelling:** Does the location meet the scene requirements and fit the director's tone?

☐ **Anachronism:** Does the setting fit the time period and story setting?

Notes:

SIGHT

○ interior   ○ exterior

[YES] [NO] **Indoor staging:** Does the crew, cast and gear fit inside?

[YES] [NO] **VFX Need:** Would anything need to be removed or added in post?

[YES] [NO] **Wide Shot test:** Wide frame acceptable?

[YES] [NO] **Wide Shot test:** Any problematicvisual elements in the frame?

[YES] [NO] **Indoor staging:** Any special production design needs?

[YES] [NO] **360 test:** Are there any problematic directions that should be avoided?

[YES] [NO] **Sunlight:** Any sunlight consideration?

[YES] [NO] **Commercial clearance:** Any properties that require commercial clearance?

○ morning   ○ noon   ○ afternoon   ○ evening   ○ night

Notes:

SOUND

[YES] [NO] **HVAC:** Can you turn off the heating, ventilation and air conditioning unit?

[YES] [NO] **Reverberation:** Can you record clean dialog?

[YES] [NO] **Refrigerators:** Can you turn off any noisy ? appliances or refrigerators?

[YES] [NO] **Reverberation:** Do you need to dampen echoes in the space?

Notes:

SURROUNDINGS

- [YES] [NO] **Roads & Traffic:** Noise or continuity issues from vehicles or pedestrians?
- [YES] [NO] **Schools:** Noise or other issues connected with students?
- [YES] [NO] **Playgrounds:** Will noise affected the sound or will people be in the frame?
- [YES] [NO] **Factories:** Any noise generated from the machines or any road issues?
- [YES] [NO] **Gas station:** Any noise or traffic issues?
- [YES] [NO] **Parking:** Is there sufficient parking for talent, crew, and production vehicles?

- [YES] [NO] **Airports:** Noise or activity and traffic issues and concerns?
- [YES] [NO] **Air traffic:** Any significant air traffic overhead and sound concerns?
- [YES] [NO] **Subway:** Will subway noise fit to the scene? Will it affect sound recording?
- [YES] [NO] **Subway:** Will subway noise fit to the scene? Will it affect sound recording?
- [YES] [NO] **Train station:** Will train noise fit in the scene? Any train appear in the frame?
- [YES] [NO] **Staging Talent:** Is there a quiet place dedicated for talent, extras, crew?
- [YES] [NO] **Restrooms:** Is there a enough restrooms for all?

Notes:

WEATHER

- [YES] [NO] **Temperature:** Is there temperature control?

- [YES] [NO] **Rain / snow:** Will precipitation have a potential impact on the shoot?
- [YES] [NO] **Indoor:** Will sound from precipitation have a potential impact on the shoot?

Notes:

POWER

[   ] How many accessible outlets?

- [YES] [NO] **Access:** Does the electrical crew has access to the circuit breaker box?
- [YES] [NO] **Hair and makeup:** Is there a dedicated space and breaker for Hair & Makeup?

FACILITIES

[   ] How many people on set to every available bathroom?

- [YES] [NO] Access to **Water Shut Off** in case of emergency
- [YES] [NO] Access to **Gas Shut Off** in case of emergency

Notes:

CONTRACTS

[YES] [NO] **Contract:** Has the location owner sign the contract/location release?

[YES] [NO] **Insurance:** Does the production insurance cover the location?

Dates needed: _____   Total number of days: _____   Total cost: _____

Contact person: _____

Phone: _____   email: _____

LOCATION SCOUTING CHECKLIST

Project:

Director:

Producer:

Location scout:

Scene: Scene Number:

Location name:

Address:

STORY

☐ **Storytelling:** Does the location meet the scene requirements and fit the director's tone?

☐ **Anachronism:** Does the setting fit the time period and story setting?

Notes:

SIGHT

○ interior   ○ exterior

[YES] [NO] **Wide Shot test:** Wide frame acceptable?

[YES] [NO] **Wide Shot test:** Any problematic visual elements in the frame?

[YES] [NO] **360 test:** Are there any problematic directions that should be avoided?

[YES] [NO] **Commercial clearance:** Any properties that require commercial clearance?

[YES] [NO] **Indoor staging:** Does the crew, cast and gear fit inside?

[YES] [NO] **VFX Need:** Would anything need to be removed or added in post?

[YES] [NO] **Indoor staging:** Any special production design needs?

[YES] [NO] **Sunlight:** Any sunlight consideration?

○ morning   ○ noon   ○ afternoon   ○ evening   ○ night

Notes:

SOUND

[YES] [NO] **HVAC:** Can you turn off the heating, ventilation and air conditioning unit?

[YES] [NO] **Refrigerators:** Can you turn off any noisy ? appliances or refrigerators?

[YES] [NO] **Reverberation:** Can you record clean dialog?

[YES] [NO] **Reverberation:** Do you need to dampen echoes in the space?

Notes:

SURROUNDINGS

[YES] [NO] **Roads & Traffic:** Noise or continuity issues from vehicles or pedestrians?

[YES] [NO] **Schools:** Noise or other issues connected with students?

[YES] [NO] **Playgrounds:** Will noise affected the sound or will people be in the frame?

[YES] [NO] **Factories:** Any noise generated from the machines or any road issues?

[YES] [NO] **Gas station:** Any noise or traffic issues?

[YES] [NO] **Parking:** Is there sufficient parking for talent, crew, and production vehicles?

[YES] [NO] **Airports:** Noise or activity and traffic issues and concerns?

[YES] [NO] **Air traffic:** Any significant air traffic overhead and sound concerns?

[YES] [NO] **Subway:** Will subway noise fit to the scene? Will it affect sound recording?

[YES] [NO] **Subway:** Will subway noise fit to the scene? Will it affect sound recording?

[YES] [NO] **Train station:** Will train noise fit in the scene? Any train appear in the frame?

[YES] [NO] **Staging Talent:** Is there a quiet place dedicated for talent, extras, crew?

[YES] [NO] **Restrooms:** Is there a enough restrooms for all?

Notes:

WEATHER

[YES] [NO] **Temperature:** Is there temperature control?

[YES] [NO] **Rain / snow:** Will precipitation have a potential impact on the shoot?

[YES] [NO] **Indoor:** Will sound from precipitation have a potential impact on the shoot?

Notes:

POWER
[ ] How many accessible outlets?

[YES] [NO] **Access:** Does the electrical crew has access to the circuit breaker box?

[YES] [NO] **Hair and makeup:** Is there a dedicated space and breaker for Hair & Makeup?

FACILITIES
[ ] How many people on set to every available bathroom?

[YES] [NO] Access to **Water Shut Off** in case of emergency

[YES] [NO] Access to **Gas Shut Off** in case of emergency

Notes:

CONTRACTS
[YES] [NO] **Contract:** Has the location owner sign the contract/location release?

[YES] [NO] **Insurance:** Does the production insurance cover the location?

Dates needed: Total number of days: Total cost:

Contact person:

Phone: email:

LOCATION SCOUTING CHECKLIST

Project:

Director:

Producer:

Location scout:

Scene: Scene Number:

Location name:

Address:

STORY

☐ **Storytelling:** Does the location meet the scene requirements and fit the director's tone?

☐ **Anachronism:** Does the setting fit the time period and story setting?

Notes:

SIGHT

○ interior   ○ exterior

YES NO	**Indoor staging:** Does the crew, cast and gear fit inside?
YES NO	**VFX Need:** Would anything need to be removed or added in post?
YES NO	**Indoor staging:** Any special production design needs?
YES NO	**Sunlight:** Any sunlight consideration?

YES NO **Wide Shot test:** Wide frame acceptable?

YES NO **Wide Shot test:** Any problematicvisual elements in the frame?

YES NO **360 test:** Are there any problematic directions that should be avoided?

YES NO **Commercial clearance:** Any properties that require commercial clearance?

○ morning   ○ noon   ○ afternoon   ○ evening   ○ night

Notes:

SOUND

YES NO **HVAC:** Can you turn off the heating, ventilation and air conditioning unit?

YES NO **Reverberation:** Can you record clean dialog?

YES NO **Refrigerators:** Can you turn off any noisy ? appliances or refrigerators?

YES NO **Reverberation:** Do you need to dampen echoes in the space?

Notes:

SURROUNDINGS

[YES] [NO] **Roads & Traffic:** Noise or continuity issues from vehicles or pedestrians?

[YES] [NO] **Schools:** Noise or other issues connected with students?

[YES] [NO] **Playgrounds:** Will noise affected the sound or will people be in the frame?

[YES] [NO] **Factories:** Any noise generated from the machines or any road issues?

[YES] [NO] **Gas station:** Any noise or traffic issues?

[YES] [NO] **Parking:** Is there sufficient parking for talent, crew, and production vehicles?

[YES] [NO] **Airports:** Noise or activity and traffic issues and concerns?

[YES] [NO] **Air traffic:** Any significant air traffic overhead and sound concerns?

[YES] [NO] **Subway:** Will subway noise fit to the scene? Will it affect sound recording?

[YES] [NO] **Subway:** Will subway noise fit to the scene? Will it affect sound recording?

[YES] [NO] **Train station:** Will train noise fit in the scene? Any train appear in the frame?

[YES] [NO] **Staging Talent:** Is there a quiet place dedicated for talent, extras, crew?

[YES] [NO] **Restrooms:** Is there a enough restrooms for all?

Notes:

WEATHER

[YES] [NO] **Temperature:** Is there temperature control?

[YES] [NO] **Rain / snow:** Will precipitation have a potential impact on the shoot?

[YES] [NO] **Indoor:** Will sound from precipitation have a potential impact on the shoot?

Notes:

POWER [   ] How many accessible outlets?

[YES] [NO] **Access:** Does the electrical crew has access to the circuit breaker box?

[YES] [NO] **Hair and makeup:** Is there a dedicated space and breaker for Hair & Makeup?

FACILITIES [   ] How many people on set to every available bathroom?

[YES] [NO] Access to **Water Shut Off** in case of emergency

[YES] [NO] Access to **Gas Shut Off** in case of emergency

Notes:

CONTRACTS [YES] [NO] **Contract:** Has the location owner sign the contract/location release?

[YES] [NO] **Insurance:** Does the production insurance cover the location?

Dates needed: Total number of days: Total cost:

Contact person:

Phone: email:

LOCATION SCOUTING CHECKLIST

Project:

Director:

Producer:

Location scout:

Scene: Scene Number:

Location name:

Address:

STORY

☐ **Storytelling:** Does the location meet the scene requirements and fit the director's tone?

☐ **Anachronism:** Does the setting fit the time period and story setting?

Notes:

SIGHT

○ interior   ○ exterior

[YES] [NO] **Wide Shot test:** Wide frame acceptable?

[YES] [NO] **Wide Shot test:** Any problematicvisual elements in the frame?

[YES] [NO] **360 test:** Are there any problematic directions that should be avoided?

[YES] [NO] **Commercial clearance:** Any properties that require commercial clearance?

[YES] [NO] **Indoor staging:** Does the crew, cast and gear fit inside?

[YES] [NO] **VFX Need:** Would anything need to be removed or added in post?

[YES] [NO] **Indoor staging:** Any special production design needs?

[YES] [NO] **Sunlight:** Any sunlight consideration?

○ morning ○ noon ○ afternoon ○ evening ○ night

Notes:

SOUND

[YES] [NO] **HVAC:** Can you turn off the heating, ventilation and air conditioning unit?

[YES] [NO] **Refrigerators:** Can you turn off any noisy ? appliances or refrigerators?

[YES] [NO] **Reverberation:** Can you record clean dialog?

[YES] [NO] **Reverberation:** Do you need to dampen echoes in the space?

Notes:

LOCATION SCOUTING CHECKLIST

SURROUNDINGS

[YES] [NO] **Roads & Traffic:** Noise or continuity issues from vehicles or pedestrians?

[YES] [NO] **Schools:** Noise or other issues connected with students?

[YES] [NO] **Playgrounds:** Will noise affected the sound or will people be in the frame?

[YES] [NO] **Factories:** Any noise generated from the machines or any road issues?

[YES] [NO] **Gas station:** Any noise or traffic issues?

[YES] [NO] **Parking:** Is there sufficient parking for talent, crew, and production vehicles?

[YES] [NO] **Airports:** Noise or activity and traffic issues and concerns?

[YES] [NO] **Air traffic:** Any significant air traffic overhead and sound concerns?

[YES] [NO] **Subway:** Will subway noise fit to the scene? Will it affect sound recording?

[YES] [NO] **Subway:** Will subway noise fit to the scene? Will it affect sound recording?

[YES] [NO] **Train station:** Will train noise fit in the scene? Any train appear in the frame?

[YES] [NO] **Staging Talent:** Is there a quiet place dedicated for talent, extras, crew?

[YES] [NO] **Restrooms:** Is there a enough restrooms for all?

Notes:

WEATHER

[YES] [NO] **Temperature:** Is there temperature control?

[YES] [NO] **Rain / snow:** Will precipitation have a potential impact on the shoot?

[YES] [NO] **Indoor:** Will sound from precipitation have a potential impact on the shoot?

Notes:

POWER [ ] How many accessible outlets?

[YES] [NO] **Access:** Does the electrical crew has access to the circuit breaker box?

[YES] [NO] **Hair and makeup:** Is there a dedicated space and breaker for Hair & Makeup?

FACILITIES [ ] How many people on set to every available bathroom?

[YES] [NO] Access to **Water Shut Off** in case of emergency

[YES] [NO] Access to **Gas Shut Off** in case of emergency

Notes:

CONTRACTS [YES] [NO] **Contract:** Has the location owner sign the contract/location release?

[YES] [NO] **Insurance:** Does the production insurance cover the location?

Dates needed: Total number of days: Total cost:

Contact person:

Phone: email:

LOCATION SCOUTING CHECKLIST

Project:

Director:

Producer:

Location scout:

Scene: Scene Number:

Location name:

Address:

STORY

☐ **Storytelling:** Does the location meet the scene requirements and fit the director's tone?

☐ **Anachronism:** Does the setting fit the time period and story setting?

Notes:

SIGHT

○ interior   ○ exterior

[YES] [NO] **Wide Shot test:** Wide frame acceptable?

[YES] [NO] **Wide Shot test:** Any problematic visual elements in the frame?

[YES] [NO] **360 test:** Are there any problematic directions that should be avoided?

[YES] [NO] **Commercial clearance:** Any properties that require commercial clearance?

[YES] [NO] **Indoor staging:** Does the crew, cast and gear fit inside?

[YES] [NO] **VFX Need:** Would anything need to be removed or added in post?

[YES] [NO] **Indoor staging:** Any special production design needs?

[YES] [NO] **Sunlight:** Any sunlight consideration?

○ morning   ○ noon   ○ afternoon   ○ evening   ○ night

Notes:

SOUND

[YES] [NO] **HVAC:** Can you turn off the heating, ventilation and air conditioning unit?

[YES] [NO] **Refrigerators:** Can you turn off any noisy ? appliances or refrigerators?

[YES] [NO] **Reverberation:** Can you record clean dialog?

[YES] [NO] **Reverberation:** Do you need to dampen echoes in the space?

Notes:

LOCATION SCOUTING CHECKLIST

SURROUNDINGS

[YES] [NO] Roads & Traffic: Noise or continuity issues from vehicles or pedestrians?

[YES] [NO] Schools: Noise or other issues connected with students?

[YES] [NO] Playgrounds: Will noise affected the sound or will people be in the frame?

[YES] [NO] Factories: Any noise generated from the machines or any road issues?

[YES] [NO] Gas station: Any noise or traffic issues?

[YES] [NO] Parking: Is there sufficient parking for talent, crew, and production vehicles?

[YES] [NO] Airports: Noise or activity and traffic issues and concerns?

[YES] [NO] Air traffic: Any significant air traffic overhead and sound concerns?

[YES] [NO] Subway: Will subway noise fit to the scene? Will it affect sound recording?

[YES] [NO] Subway: Will subway noise fit to the scene? Will it affect sound recording?

[YES] [NO] Train station: Will train noise fit in the scene? Any train appear in the frame?

[YES] [NO] Staging Talent: Is there a quiet place dedicated for talent, extras, crew?

[YES] [NO] Restrooms: Is there a enough restrooms for all?

Notes:

WEATHER

[YES] [NO] Temperature: Is there temperature control?

[YES] [NO] Rain / snow: Will precipitation have a potential impact on the shoot?

[YES] [NO] Indoor: Will sound from precipitation have a potential impact on the shoot?

Notes:

POWER [   ] How many accessible outlets?

[YES] [NO] Access: Does the electrical crew has access to the circuit breaker box?

[YES] [NO] Hair and makeup: Is there a dedicated space and breaker for Hair & Makeup?

FACILITIES [   ] How many people on set to every available bathroom?

[YES] [NO] Access to **Water Shut Off** in case of emergency

[YES] [NO] Access to **Gas Shut Off** in case of emergency

Notes:

CONTRACTS [YES] [NO] Contract: Has the location owner sign the contract/location release?

[YES] [NO] Insurance: Does the production insurance cover the location?

Dates needed: _____ Total number of days: _____ Total cost: _____

Contact person: _____

Phone: _____ email: _____

LOCATION SCOUTING CHECKLIST

Project:

Director:

Producer:

Location scout:

Scene: Scene Number:

Location name:

Address:

STORY

☐ **Storytelling:** Does the location meet the scene requirements and fit the director's tone?

☐ **Anachronism:** Does the setting fit the time period and story setting?

Notes:

SIGHT

◯ interior   ◯ exterior

[YES] [NO] **Wide Shot test:** Wide frame acceptable?

[YES] [NO] **Wide Shot test:** Any problematicvisual elements in the frame?

[YES] [NO] **360 test:** Are there any problematic directions that should be avoided?

[YES] [NO] **Commercial clearance:** Any properties that require commercial clearance?

[YES] [NO] **Indoor staging:** Does the crew, cast and gear fit inside?

[YES] [NO] **VFX Need:** Would anything need to be removed or added in post?

[YES] [NO] **Indoor staging:** Any special production design needs?

[YES] [NO] **Sunlight:** Any sunlight consideration?

◯ morning   ◯ noon   ◯ afternoon   ◯ evening   ◯ night

Notes:

SOUND

[YES] [NO] **HVAC:** Can you turn off the heating, ventilation and air conditioning unit?

[YES] [NO] **Refrigerators:** Can you turn off any noisy ? appliances or refrigerators?

[YES] [NO] **Reverberation:** Can you record clean dialog?

[YES] [NO] **Reverberation:** Do you need to dampen echoes in the space?

Notes:

LOCATION SCOUTING CHECKLIST

SURROUNDINGS

[YES] [NO] **Roads & Traffic:** Noise or continuity issues from vehicles or pedestrians?

[YES] [NO] **Schools:** Noise or other issues connected with students?

[YES] [NO] **Playgrounds:** Will noise affected the sound or will people be in the frame?

[YES] [NO] **Factories:** Any noise generated from the machines or any road issues?

[YES] [NO] **Gas station:** Any noise or traffic issues?

[YES] [NO] **Parking:** Is there sufficient parking for talent, crew, and production vehicles?

[YES] [NO] **Airports:** Noise or activity and traffic issues and concerns?

[YES] [NO] **Air traffic:** Any significant air traffic overhead and sound concerns?

[YES] [NO] **Subway:** Will subway noise fit to the scene? Will it affect sound recording?

[YES] [NO] **Subway:** Will subway noise fit to the scene? Will it affect sound recording?

[YES] [NO] **Train station:** Will train noise fit in the scene? Any train appear in the frame?

[YES] [NO] **Staging Talent:** Is there a quiet place dedicated for talent, extras, crew?

[YES] [NO] **Restrooms:** Is there a enough restrooms for all?

Notes:

WEATHER

[YES] [NO] **Temperature:** Is there temperature control?

[YES] [NO] **Rain / snow:** Will precipitation have a potential impact on the shoot?

[YES] [NO] **Indoor:** Will sound from precipitation have a potential impact on the shoot?

Notes:

POWER

[   ] How many accessible outlets?

[YES] [NO] **Access:** Does the electrical crew has access to the circuit breaker box?

[YES] [NO] **Hair and makeup:** Is there a dedicated space and breaker for Hair & Makeup?

FACILITIES

[   ] How many people on set to every available bathroom?

[YES] [NO] **Access to Water Shut Off** in case of emergency

[YES] [NO] **Access to Gas Shut Off** in case of emergency

Notes:

CONTRACTS

[YES] [NO] **Contract:** Has the location owner sign the contract/location release?

[YES] [NO] **Insurance:** Does the production insurance cover the location?

Dates needed: **Total number of days:**   **Total cost:**

Contact person:

Phone: **email:**

LOCATION SCOUTING CHECKLIST

Project:

Director:

Producer:

Location scout:

Scene: Scene Number:

Location name:

Address:

STORY

☐ **Storytelling:** Does the location meet the scene requirements and fit the director's tone?

☐ **Anachronism:** Does the setting fit the time period and story setting?

Notes:

SIGHT

◯ interior   ◯ exterior

| YES | NO | **Indoor staging:** Does the crew, cast and gear fit inside? |

| YES | NO | **VFX Need:** Would anything need to be removed or added in post? |

| YES | NO | **Wide Shot test:** Wide frame acceptable? |

| YES | NO | **Wide Shot test:** Any problematicvisual elements in the frame? |

| YES | NO | **Indoor staging:** Any special production design needs? |

| YES | NO | **360 test:** Are there any problematic directions that should be avoided? |

| YES | NO | **Sunlight:** Any sunlight consideration? |

| YES | NO | **Commercial clearance:** Any properties that require commercial clearance? |

◯ morning   ◯ noon   ◯ afternoon   ◯ evening   ◯ night

Notes:

SOUND

| YES | NO | **HVAC:** Can you turn off the heating, ventilation and air conditioning unit? |

| YES | NO | **Reverberation:** Can you record clean dialog? |

| YES | NO | **Refrigerators:** Can you turn off any noisy ? appliances or refrigerators? |

| YES | NO | **Reverberation:** Do you need to dampen echoes in the space? |

Notes:

LOCATION SCOUTING CHECKLIST

SURROUNDINGS

YES **NO** **Roads & Traffic:** Noise or continuity issues from vehicles or pedestrians?

YES **NO** **Schools:** Noise or other issues connected with students?

YES **NO** **Playgrounds:** Will noise affected the sound or will people be in the frame?

YES **NO** **Factories:** Any noise generated from the machines or any road issues?

YES **NO** **Gas station:** Any noise or traffic issues?

YES **NO** **Parking:** Is there sufficient parking for talent, crew, and production vehicles?

YES **NO** **Airports:** Noise or activity and traffic issues and concerns?

YES **NO** **Air traffic:** Any significant air traffic overhead and sound concerns?

YES **NO** **Subway:** Will subway noise fit to the scene? Will it affect sound recording?

YES **NO** **Subway:** Will subway noise fit to the scene? Will it affect sound recording?

YES **NO** **Train station:** Will train noise fit in the scene? Any train appear in the frame?

YES **NO** **Staging Talent:** Is there a quiet place dedicated for talent, extras, crew?

YES **NO** **Restrooms:** Is there a enough restrooms for all?

Notes:

WEATHER

YES **NO** **Temperature:** Is there temperature control?

YES **NO** **Rain / snow:** Will precipitation have a potential impact on the shoot?

YES **NO** **Indoor:** Will sound from precipitation have a potential impact on the shoot?

Notes:

POWER

☐ How many accessible outlets?

YES **NO** **Access:** Does the electrical crew has access to the circuit breaker box?

YES **NO** **Hair and makeup:** Is there a dedicated space and breaker for Hair & Makeup?

FACILITIES

☐ How many people on set to every available bathroom?

YES **NO** Access to **Water Shut Off** in case of emergency

YES **NO** Access to **Gas Shut Off** in case of emergency

Notes:

CONTRACTS

YES **NO** **Contract:** Has the location owner sign the contract/location release?

YES **NO** **Insurance:** Does the production insurance cover the location?

Dates needed: _____

Total number of days: _____

Total cost: _____

Contact person: _____

Phone: _____

email: _____

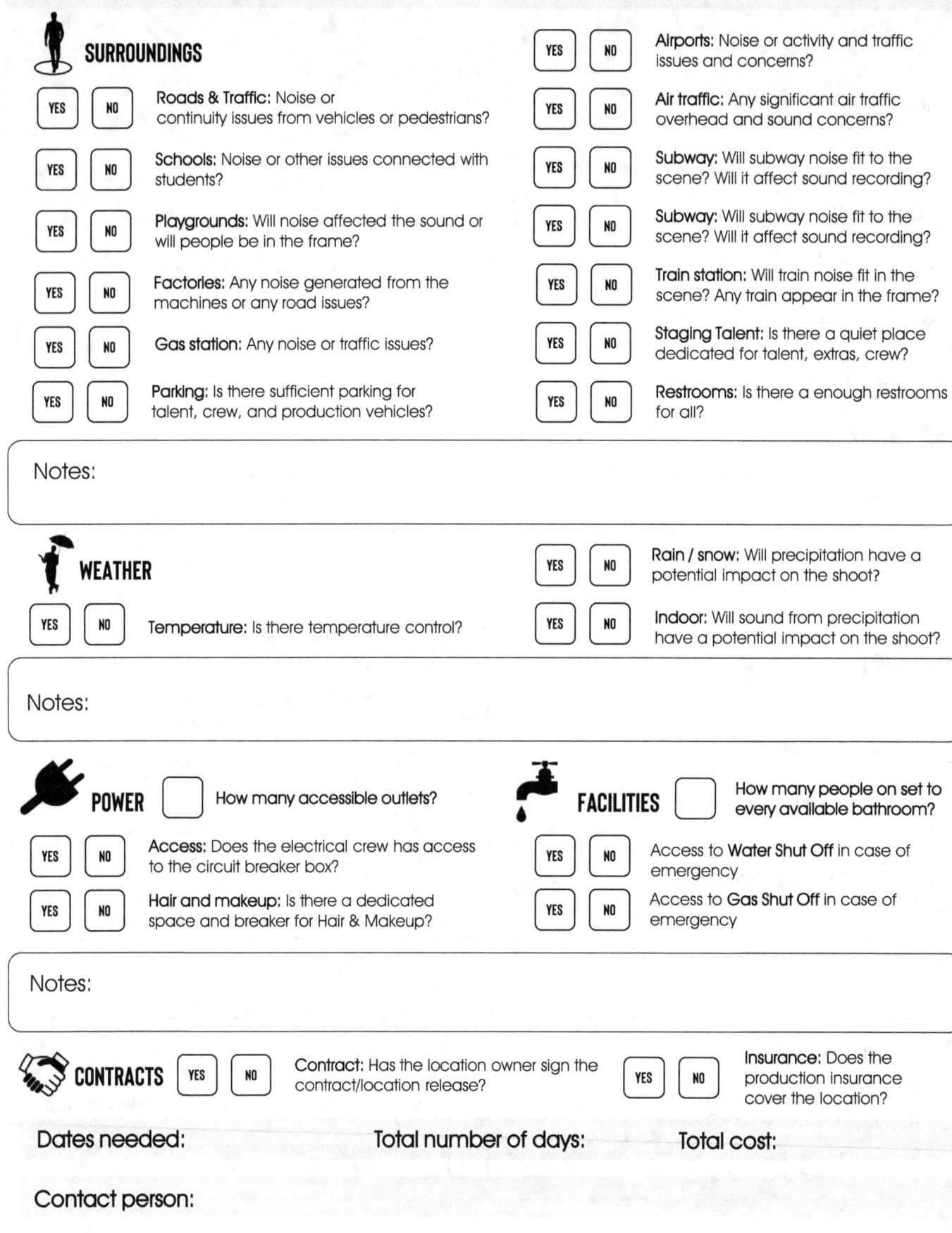

Project:

Director:

Producer:

Location scout:

Scene: Scene Number:

Location name:

Address:

STORY

☐ **Storytelling:** Does the location meet the scene requirements and fit the director's tone?

☐ **Anachronism:** Does the setting fit the time period and story setting?

Notes:

SIGHT

○ interior   ○ exterior

[YES] [NO] **Wide Shot test:** Wide frame acceptable?

[YES] [NO] **Wide Shot test:** Any problematicvisual elements in the frame?

[YES] [NO] **360 test:** Are there any problematic directions that should be avoided?

[YES] [NO] **Commercial clearance:** Any properties that require commercial clearance?

[YES] [NO] **Indoor staging:** Does the crew, cast and gear fit inside?

[YES] [NO] **VFX Need:** Would anything need to be removed or added in post?

[YES] [NO] **Indoor staging:** Any special production design needs?

[YES] [NO] **Sunlight:** Any sunlight consideration?

○ morning ○ noon ○ afternoon ○ evening ○ night

Notes:

SOUND

[YES] [NO] **HVAC:** Can you turn off the heating, ventilation and air conditioning unit?

[YES] [NO] **Refrigerators:** Can you turn off any noisy ? appliances or refrigerators?

[YES] [NO] **Reverberation:** Can you record clean dialog?

[YES] [NO] **Reverberation:** Do you need to dampen echoes in the space?

Notes:

LOCATION SCOUTING CHECKLIST

SURROUNDINGS

[YES] [NO] **Roads & Traffic:** Noise or continuity issues from vehicles or pedestrians?

[YES] [NO] **Schools:** Noise or other issues connected with students?

[YES] [NO] **Playgrounds:** Will noise affected the sound or will people be in the frame?

[YES] [NO] **Factories:** Any noise generated from the machines or any road issues?

[YES] [NO] **Gas station:** Any noise or traffic issues?

[YES] [NO] **Parking:** Is there sufficient parking for talent, crew, and production vehicles?

[YES] [NO] **Airports:** Noise or activity and traffic issues and concerns?

[YES] [NO] **Air traffic:** Any significant air traffic overhead and sound concerns?

[YES] [NO] **Subway:** Will subway noise fit to the scene? Will it affect sound recording?

[YES] [NO] **Subway:** Will subway noise fit to the scene? Will it affect sound recording?

[YES] [NO] **Train station:** Will train noise fit in the scene? Any train appear in the frame?

[YES] [NO] **Staging Talent:** Is there a quiet place dedicated for talent, extras, crew?

[YES] [NO] **Restrooms:** Is there a enough restrooms for all?

Notes:

WEATHER

[YES] [NO] **Temperature:** Is there temperature control?

[YES] [NO] **Rain / snow:** Will precipitation have a potential impact on the shoot?

[YES] [NO] **Indoor:** Will sound from precipitation have a potential impact on the shoot?

Notes:

POWER

[ ] How many accessible outlets?

[YES] [NO] **Access:** Does the electrical crew has access to the circuit breaker box?

[YES] [NO] **Hair and makeup:** Is there a dedicated space and breaker for Hair & Makeup?

FACILITIES

[ ] How many people on set to every available bathroom?

[YES] [NO] Access to **Water Shut Off** in case of emergency

[YES] [NO] Access to **Gas Shut Off** in case of emergency

Notes:

CONTRACTS

[YES] [NO] **Contract:** Has the location owner sign the contract/location release?

[YES] [NO] **Insurance:** Does the production insurance cover the location?

Dates needed: Total number of days: Total cost:

Contact person:

Phone: email:

LOCATION SCOUTING CHECKLIST

Project:

Director:

Producer:

Location scout:

Scene: Scene Number:

Location name:

Address:

STORY

☐ **Storytelling:** Does the location meet the scene requirements and fit the director's tone?

☐ **Anachronism:** Does the setting fit the time period and story setting?

Notes:

SIGHT

○ interior   ○ exterior

☐ YES ☐ NO **Wide Shot test:** Wide frame acceptable?

☐ YES ☐ NO **Wide Shot test:** Any problematic visual elements in the frame?

☐ YES ☐ NO **360 test:** Are there any problematic directions that should be avoided?

☐ YES ☐ NO **Commercial clearance:** Any properties that require commercial clearance?

☐ YES ☐ NO **Indoor staging:** Does the crew, cast and gear fit inside?

☐ YES ☐ NO **VFX Need:** Would anything need to be removed or added in post?

☐ YES ☐ NO **Indoor staging:** Any special production design needs?

☐ YES ☐ NO **Sunlight:** Any sunlight consideration?

○ morning ○ noon ○ afternoon ○ evening ○ night

Notes:

SOUND

☐ YES ☐ NO **HVAC:** Can you turn off the heating, ventilation and air conditioning unit?

☐ YES ☐ NO **Refrigerators:** Can you turn off any noisy ? appliances or refrigerators?

☐ YES ☐ NO **Reverberation:** Can you record clean dialog?

☐ YES ☐ NO **Reverberation:** Do you need to dampen echoes in the space?

Notes:

SURROUNDINGS

Roads & Traffic: Noise or continuity issues from vehicles or pedestrians? YES NO

Schools: Noise or other issues connected with students? YES NO

Playgrounds: Will noise affected the sound or will people be in the frame? YES NO

Factories: Any noise generated from the machines or any road issues? YES NO

Gas station: Any noise or traffic issues? YES NO

Parking: Is there sufficient parking for talent, crew, and production vehicles? YES NO

Airports: Noise or activity and traffic issues and concerns? YES NO

Air traffic: Any significant air traffic overhead and sound concerns? YES NO

Subway: Will subway noise fit to the scene? Will it affect sound recording? YES NO

Subway: Will subway noise fit to the scene? Will it affect sound recording? YES NO

Train station: Will train noise fit in the scene? Any train appear in the frame? YES NO

Staging Talent: Is there a quiet place dedicated for talent, extras, crew? YES NO

Restrooms: Is there a enough restrooms for all? YES NO

Notes:

WEATHER

Temperature: Is there temperature control? YES NO

Rain / snow: Will precipitation have a potential impact on the shoot? YES NO

Indoor: Will sound from precipitation have a potential impact on the shoot? YES NO

Notes:

POWER

How many accessible outlets?

Access: Does the electrical crew has access to the circuit breaker box? YES NO

Hair and makeup: Is there a dedicated space and breaker for Hair & Makeup? YES NO

FACILITIES

How many people on set to every available bathroom?

Access to **Water Shut Off** in case of emergency YES NO

Access to **Gas Shut Off** in case of emergency YES NO

Notes:

CONTRACTS

Contract: Has the location owner sign the contract/location release? YES NO

Insurance: Does the production insurance cover the location? YES NO

Dates needed:

Total number of days:

Total cost:

Contact person:

Phone:

email:

LOCATION SCOUTING CHECKLIST

Project:

Director:

Producer:

Location scout:

Scene: Scene Number:

Location name:

Address:

STORY

☐ **Storytelling:** Does the location meet the scene requirements and fit the director's tone?

☐ **Anachronism:** Does the setting fit the time period and story setting?

Notes:

SIGHT

○ interior   ○ exterior

[YES] [NO] **Wide Shot test:** Wide frame acceptable?

[YES] [NO] **Wide Shot test:** Any problematicvisual elements in the frame?

[YES] [NO] **360 test:** Are there any problematic directions that should be avoided?

[YES] [NO] **Commercial clearance:** Any properties that require commercial clearance?

[YES] [NO] **Indoor staging:** Does the crew, cast and gear fit inside?

[YES] [NO] **VFX Need:** Would anything need to be removed or added in post?

[YES] [NO] **Indoor staging:** Any special production design needs?

[YES] [NO] **Sunlight:** Any sunlight consideration?

○ morning   ○ noon   ○ afternoon   ○ evening   ○ night

Notes:

SOUND

[YES] [NO] **HVAC:** Can you turn off the heating, ventilation and air conditioning unit?

[YES] [NO] **Refrigerators:** Can you turn off any noisy ? appliances or refrigerators?

[YES] [NO] **Reverberation:** Can you record clean dialog?

[YES] [NO] **Reverberation:** Do you need to dampen echoes in the space?

Notes:

SURROUNDINGS

YES | NO — **Roads & Traffic:** Noise or continuity issues from vehicles or pedestrians?

YES | NO — **Schools:** Noise or other issues connected with students?

YES | NO — **Playgrounds:** Will noise affected the sound or will people be in the frame?

YES | NO — **Factories:** Any noise generated from the machines or any road issues?

YES | NO — **Gas station:** Any noise or traffic issues?

YES | NO — **Parking:** Is there sufficient parking for talent, crew, and production vehicles?

YES | NO — **Airports:** Noise or activity and traffic issues and concerns?

YES | NO — **Air traffic:** Any significant air traffic overhead and sound concerns?

YES | NO — **Subway:** Will subway noise fit to the scene? Will it affect sound recording?

YES | NO — **Subway:** Will subway noise fit to the scene? Will it affect sound recording?

YES | NO — **Train station:** Will train noise fit in the scene? Any train appear in the frame?

YES | NO — **Staging Talent:** Is there a quiet place dedicated for talent, extras, crew?

YES | NO — **Restrooms:** Is there a enough restrooms for all?

Notes:

WEATHER

YES | NO — **Temperature:** Is there temperature control?

YES | NO — **Rain / snow:** Will precipitation have a potential impact on the shoot?

YES | NO — **Indoor:** Will sound from precipitation have a potential impact on the shoot?

Notes:

POWER

[ ] How many accessible outlets?

YES | NO — **Access:** Does the electrical crew has access to the circuit breaker box?

YES | NO — **Hair and makeup:** Is there a dedicated space and breaker for Hair & Makeup?

FACILITIES

[ ] How many people on set to every available bathroom?

YES | NO — Access to **Water Shut Off** in case of emergency

YES | NO — Access to **Gas Shut Off** in case of emergency

Notes:

CONTRACTS

YES | NO — **Contract:** Has the location owner sign the contract/location release?

YES | NO — **Insurance:** Does the production insurance cover the location?

Dates needed: Total number of days: Total cost:

Contact person:

Phone: email:

LOCATION SCOUTING CHECKLIST

Project:

Director:

Producer:

Location scout:

Scene: Scene Number:

Location name:

Address:

STORY

[ ] **Storytelling:** Does the location meet the scene requirements and fit the director's tone?

[ ] **Anachronism:** Does the setting fit the time period and story setting?

Notes:

SIGHT

( ) interior   ( ) exterior

[YES] [NO] **Wide Shot test:** Wide frame acceptable?

[YES] [NO] **Wide Shot test:** Any problematicvisual elements in the frame?

[YES] [NO] **360 test:** Are there any problematic directions that should be avoided?

[YES] [NO] **Commercial clearance:** Any properties that require commercial clearance?

[YES] [NO] **Indoor staging:** Does the crew, cast and gear fit inside?

[YES] [NO] **VFX Need:** Would anything need to be removed or added in post?

[YES] [NO] **Indoor staging:** Any special production design needs?

[YES] [NO] **Sunlight:** Any sunlight consideration?

( ) morning   ( ) noon   ( ) afternoon   ( ) evening   ( ) night

Notes:

SOUND

[YES] [NO] **HVAC:** Can you turn off the heating, ventilation and air conditioning unit?

[YES] [NO] **Refrigerators:** Can you turn off any noisy ? appliances or refrigerators?

[YES] [NO] **Reverberation:** Can you record clean dialog?

[YES] [NO] **Reverberation:** Do you need to dampen echoes in the space?

Notes:

SURROUNDINGS

[YES] [NO] **Roads & Traffic:** Noise or continuity issues from vehicles or pedestrians?

[YES] [NO] **Schools:** Noise or other issues connected with students?

[YES] [NO] **Playgrounds:** Will noise affected the sound or will people be in the frame?

[YES] [NO] **Factories:** Any noise generated from the machines or any road issues?

[YES] [NO] **Gas station:** Any noise or traffic issues?

[YES] [NO] **Parking:** Is there sufficient parking for talent, crew, and production vehicles?

[YES] [NO] **Airports:** Noise or activity and traffic issues and concerns?

[YES] [NO] **Air traffic:** Any significant air traffic overhead and sound concerns?

[YES] [NO] **Subway:** Will subway noise fit to the scene? Will it affect sound recording?

[YES] [NO] **Subway:** Will subway noise fit to the scene? Will it affect sound recording?

[YES] [NO] **Train station:** Will train noise fit in the scene? Any train appear in the frame?

[YES] [NO] **Staging Talent:** Is there a quiet place dedicated for talent, extras, crew?

[YES] [NO] **Restrooms:** Is there a enough restrooms for all?

Notes:

WEATHER

[YES] [NO] **Temperature:** Is there temperature control?

[YES] [NO] **Rain / snow:** Will precipitation have a potential impact on the shoot?

[YES] [NO] **Indoor:** Will sound from precipitation have a potential impact on the shoot?

Notes:

POWER

[ ] How many accessible outlets?

[YES] [NO] **Access:** Does the electrical crew has access to the circuit breaker box?

[YES] [NO] **Hair and makeup:** Is there a dedicated space and breaker for Hair & Makeup?

FACILITIES

[ ] How many people on set to every available bathroom?

[YES] [NO] Access to **Water Shut Off** in case of emergency

[YES] [NO] Access to **Gas Shut Off** in case of emergency

Notes:

CONTRACTS

[YES] [NO] **Contract:** Has the location owner sign the contract/location release?

[YES] [NO] **Insurance:** Does the production insurance cover the location?

Dates needed: Total number of days: Total cost:

Contact person:

Phone: email:

LOCATION SCOUTING CHECKLIST

Project:

Director:

Producer:

Location scout:

Scene: Scene Number:

Location name:

Address:

STORY

☐ **Storytelling:** Does the location meet the scene requirements and fit the director's tone?

☐ **Anachronism:** Does the setting fit the time period and story setting?

Notes:

SIGHT

○ interior   ○ exterior

☐ YES ☐ NO **Wide Shot test:** Wide frame acceptable?

☐ YES ☐ NO **Wide Shot test:** Any problematicvisual elements in the frame?

☐ YES ☐ NO **360 test:** Are there any problematic directions that should be avoided?

☐ YES ☐ NO **Commercial clearance:** Any properties that require commercial clearance?

☐ YES ☐ NO **Indoor staging:** Does the crew, cast and gear fit inside?

☐ YES ☐ NO **VFX Need:** Would anything need to be removed or added in post?

☐ YES ☐ NO **Indoor staging:** Any special production design needs?

☐ YES ☐ NO **Sunlight:** Any sunlight consideration?

○ morning   ○ noon   ○ afternoon   ○ evening   ○ night

Notes:

SOUND

☐ YES ☐ NO **HVAC:** Can you turn off the heating, ventilation and air conditioning unit?

☐ YES ☐ NO **Refrigerators:** Can you turn off any noisy ? appliances or refrigerators?

☐ YES ☐ NO **Reverberation:** Can you record clean dialog?

☐ YES ☐ NO **Reverberation:** Do you need to dampen echoes in the space?

Notes:

LOCATION SCOUTING CHECKLIST

SURROUNDINGS

YES **NO** — **Roads & Traffic:** Noise or continuity issues from vehicles or pedestrians?

YES **NO** — **Schools:** Noise or other issues connected with students?

YES **NO** — **Playgrounds:** Will noise affected the sound or will people be in the frame?

YES **NO** — **Factories:** Any noise generated from the machines or any road issues?

YES **NO** — **Gas station:** Any noise or traffic issues?

YES **NO** — **Parking:** Is there sufficient parking for talent, crew, and production vehicles?

YES **NO** — **Airports:** Noise or activity and traffic issues and concerns?

YES **NO** — **Air traffic:** Any significant air traffic overhead and sound concerns?

YES **NO** — **Subway:** Will subway noise fit to the scene? Will it affect sound recording?

YES **NO** — **Subway:** Will subway noise fit to the scene? Will it affect sound recording?

YES **NO** — **Train station:** Will train noise fit in the scene? Any train appear in the frame?

YES **NO** — **Staging Talent:** Is there a quiet place dedicated for talent, extras, crew?

YES **NO** — **Restrooms:** Is there a enough restrooms for all?

Notes:

WEATHER

YES **NO** — **Temperature:** Is there temperature control?

YES **NO** — **Rain / snow:** Will precipitation have a potential impact on the shoot?

YES **NO** — **Indoor:** Will sound from precipitation have a potential impact on the shoot?

Notes:

POWER

[ ] How many accessible outlets?

YES **NO** — **Access:** Does the electrical crew has access to the circuit breaker box?

YES **NO** — **Hair and makeup:** Is there a dedicated space and breaker for Hair & Makeup?

FACILITIES

[ ] How many people on set to every available bathroom?

YES **NO** — Access to **Water Shut Off** in case of emergency

YES **NO** — Access to **Gas Shut Off** in case of emergency

Notes:

CONTRACTS

YES **NO** — **Contract:** Has the location owner sign the contract/location release?

YES **NO** — **Insurance:** Does the production insurance cover the location?

Dates needed: Total number of days: Total cost:

Contact person:

Phone: email:

LOCATION SCOUTING CHECKLIST

Project:

Director:

Producer:

Location scout:

Scene: Scene Number:

Location name:

Address:

STORY

☐ **Storytelling:** Does the location meet the scene requirements and fit the director's tone?

☐ **Anachronism:** Does the setting fit the time period and story setting?

Notes:

SIGHT

○ interior   ○ exterior

YES NO **Wide Shot test:** Wide frame acceptable?

YES NO **Wide Shot test:** Any problematicvisual elements in the frame?

YES NO **360 test:** Are there any problematic directions that should be avoided?

YES NO **Commercial clearance:** Any properties that require commercial clearance?

YES NO **Indoor staging:** Does the crew, cast and gear fit inside?

YES NO **VFX Need:** Would anything need to be removed or added in post?

YES NO **Indoor staging:** Any special production design needs?

YES NO **Sunlight:** Any sunlight consideration?

○ morning   ○ noon   ○ afternoon   ○ evening   ○ night

Notes:

SOUND

YES NO **HVAC:** Can you turn off the heating, ventilation and air conditioning unit?

YES NO **Refrigerators:** Can you turn off any noisy ? appliances or refrigerators?

YES NO **Reverberation:** Can you record clean dialog?

YES NO **Reverberation:** Do you need to dampen echoes in the space?

Notes:

LOCATION SCOUTING CHECKLIST

SURROUNDINGS

YES	NO	
YES	NO	**Roads & Traffic:** Noise or continuity issues from vehicles or pedestrians?
YES	NO	**Schools:** Noise or other issues connected with students?
YES	NO	**Playgrounds:** Will noise affected the sound or will people be in the frame?
YES	NO	**Factories:** Any noise generated from the machines or any road issues?
YES	NO	**Gas station:** Any noise or traffic issues?
YES	NO	**Parking:** Is there sufficient parking for talent, crew, and production vehicles?

YES	NO	
YES	NO	**Airports:** Noise or activity and traffic issues and concerns?
YES	NO	**Air traffic:** Any significant air traffic overhead and sound concerns?
YES	NO	**Subway:** Will subway noise fit to the scene? Will it affect sound recording?
YES	NO	**Subway:** Will subway noise fit to the scene? Will it affect sound recording?
YES	NO	**Train station:** Will train noise fit in the scene? Any train appear in the frame?
YES	NO	**Staging Talent:** Is there a quiet place dedicated for talent, extras, crew?
YES	NO	**Restrooms:** Is there a enough restrooms for all?

Notes:

WEATHER

YES	NO	
YES	NO	**Temperature:** Is there temperature control?

YES	NO	
YES	NO	**Rain / snow:** Will precipitation have a potential impact on the shoot?
YES	NO	**Indoor:** Will sound from precipitation have a potential impact on the shoot?

Notes:

POWER

[ ] How many accessible outlets?

YES	NO	
YES	NO	**Access:** Does the electrical crew has access to the circuit breaker box?
YES	NO	**Hair and makeup:** Is there a dedicated space and breaker for Hair & Makeup?

FACILITIES

[ ] How many people on set to every available bathroom?

YES	NO	
YES	NO	Access to **Water Shut Off** in case of emergency
YES	NO	Access to **Gas Shut Off** in case of emergency

Notes:

CONTRACTS

YES	NO	
YES	NO	**Contract:** Has the location owner sign the contract/location release?

YES	NO	
YES	NO	**Insurance:** Does the production insurance cover the location?

Dates needed: Total number of days: Total cost:

Contact person:

Phone: email:

LOCATION SCOUTING CHECKLIST

Project:

Director:

Producer:

Location scout:

Scene: Scene Number:

Location name:

Address:

STORY

☐ **Storytelling:** Does the location meet the scene requirements and fit the director's tone?

☐ **Anachronism:** Does the setting fit the time period and story setting?

Notes:

SIGHT

○ interior   ○ exterior

☐ YES ☐ NO **Wide Shot test:** Wide frame acceptable?

☐ YES ☐ NO **Wide Shot test:** Any problematicvisual elements in the frame?

☐ YES ☐ NO **360 test:** Are there any problematic directions that should be avoided?

☐ YES ☐ NO **Commercial clearance:** Any properties that require commercial clearance?

☐ YES ☐ NO **Indoor staging:** Does the crew, cast and gear fit inside?

☐ YES ☐ NO **VFX Need:** Would anything need to be removed or added in post?

☐ YES ☐ NO **Indoor staging:** Any special production design needs?

☐ YES ☐ NO **Sunlight:** Any sunlight consideration?

○ morning   ○ noon   ○ afternoon   ○ evening   ○ night

Notes:

SOUND

☐ YES ☐ NO **HVAC:** Can you turn off the heating, ventilation and air conditioning unit?

☐ YES ☐ NO **Refrigerators:** Can you turn off any noisy ? appliances or refrigerators?

☐ YES ☐ NO **Reverberation:** Can you record clean dialog?

☐ YES ☐ NO **Reverberation:** Do you need to dampen echoes in the space?

Notes:

LOCATION SCOUTING CHECKLIST

SURROUNDINGS

[YES] [NO]   **Roads & Traffic:** Noise or continuity issues from vehicles or pedestrians?

[YES] [NO]   **Schools:** Noise or other issues connected with students?

[YES] [NO]   **Playgrounds:** Will noise affected the sound or will people be in the frame?

[YES] [NO]   **Factories:** Any noise generated from the machines or any road issues?

[YES] [NO]   **Gas station:** Any noise or traffic issues?

[YES] [NO]   **Parking:** Is there sufficient parking for talent, crew, and production vehicles?

[YES] [NO]   **Airports:** Noise or activity and traffic issues and concerns?

[YES] [NO]   **Air traffic:** Any significant air traffic overhead and sound concerns?

[YES] [NO]   **Subway:** Will subway noise fit to the scene? Will it affect sound recording?

[YES] [NO]   **Subway:** Will subway noise fit to the scene? Will it affect sound recording?

[YES] [NO]   **Train station:** Will train noise fit in the scene? Any train appear in the frame?

[YES] [NO]   **Staging Talent:** Is there a quiet place dedicated for talent, extras, crew?

[YES] [NO]   **Restrooms:** Is there a enough restrooms for all?

Notes:

WEATHER

[YES] [NO]   **Temperature:** Is there temperature control?

[YES] [NO]   **Rain / snow:** Will precipitation have a potential impact on the shoot?

[YES] [NO]   **Indoor:** Will sound from precipitation have a potential impact on the shoot?

Notes:

POWER

[   ] How many accessible outlets?

[YES] [NO]   **Access:** Does the electrical crew has access to the circuit breaker box?

[YES] [NO]   **Hair and makeup:** Is there a dedicated space and breaker for Hair & Makeup?

FACILITIES

[   ] How many people on set to every available bathroom?

[YES] [NO]   Access to **Water Shut Off** in case of emergency

[YES] [NO]   Access to **Gas Shut Off** in case of emergency

Notes:

CONTRACTS

[YES] [NO]   **Contract:** Has the location owner sign the contract/location release?

[YES] [NO]   **Insurance:** Does the production insurance cover the location?

Dates needed: Total number of days: Total cost:

Contact person:

Phone: email:

LOCATION SCOUTING CHECKLIST

Project:

Director:

Producer:

Location scout:

Scene: Scene Number:

Location name:

Address:

STORY

☐ **Storytelling:** Does the location meet the scene requirements and fit the director's tone?

☐ **Anachronism:** Does the setting fit the time period and story setting?

Notes:

SIGHT

○ interior   ○ exterior

☐ YES ☐ NO **Wide Shot test:** Wide frame acceptable?

☐ YES ☐ NO **Wide Shot test:** Any problematicvisual elements in the frame?

☐ YES ☐ NO **360 test:** Are there any problematic directions that should be avoided?

☐ YES ☐ NO **Commercial clearance:** Any properties that require commercial clearance?

☐ YES ☐ NO **Indoor staging:** Does the crew, cast and gear fit inside?

☐ YES ☐ NO **VFX Need:** Would anything need to be removed or added in post?

☐ YES ☐ NO **Indoor staging:** Any special production design needs?

☐ YES ☐ NO **Sunlight:** Any sunlight consideration?

○ morning   ○ noon   ○ afternoon   ○ evening   ○ night

Notes:

SOUND

☐ YES ☐ NO **HVAC:** Can you turn off the heating, ventilation and air conditioning unit?

☐ YES ☐ NO **Refrigerators:** Can you turn off any noisy ? appliances or refrigerators?

☐ YES ☐ NO **Reverberation:** Can you record clean dialog?

☐ YES ☐ NO **Reverberation:** Do you need to dampen echoes in the space?

Notes:

SURROUNDINGS

[YES] [NO] **Roads & Traffic:** Noise or continuity issues from vehicles or pedestrians?

[YES] [NO] **Schools:** Noise or other issues connected with students?

[YES] [NO] **Playgrounds:** Will noise affected the sound or will people be in the frame?

[YES] [NO] **Factories:** Any noise generated from the machines or any road issues?

[YES] [NO] **Gas station:** Any noise or traffic issues?

[YES] [NO] **Parking:** Is there sufficient parking for talent, crew, and production vehicles?

[YES] [NO] **Airports:** Noise or activity and traffic issues and concerns?

[YES] [NO] **Air traffic:** Any significant air traffic overhead and sound concerns?

[YES] [NO] **Subway:** Will subway noise fit to the scene? Will it affect sound recording?

[YES] [NO] **Subway:** Will subway noise fit to the scene? Will it affect sound recording?

[YES] [NO] **Train station:** Will train noise fit in the scene? Any train appear in the frame?

[YES] [NO] **Staging Talent:** Is there a quiet place dedicated for talent, extras, crew?

[YES] [NO] **Restrooms:** Is there a enough restrooms for all?

Notes:

WEATHER

[YES] [NO] **Temperature:** Is there temperature control?

[YES] [NO] **Rain / snow:** Will precipitation have a potential impact on the shoot?

[YES] [NO] **Indoor:** Will sound from precipitation have a potential impact on the shoot?

Notes:

POWER

[ ] How many accessible outlets?

[YES] [NO] **Access:** Does the electrical crew has access to the circuit breaker box?

[YES] [NO] **Hair and makeup:** Is there a dedicated space and breaker for Hair & Makeup?

FACILITIES

[ ] How many people on set to every available bathroom?

[YES] [NO] Access to **Water Shut Off** in case of emergency

[YES] [NO] Access to **Gas Shut Off** in case of emergency

Notes:

CONTRACTS

[YES] [NO] **Contract:** Has the location owner sign the contract/location release?

[YES] [NO] **Insurance:** Does the production insurance cover the location?

Dates needed: Total number of days: Total cost:

Contact person:

Phone: email:

LOCATION SCOUTING CHECKLIST

Project:

Director:

Producer:

Location scout:

Scene: Scene Number:

Location name:

Address:

STORY

☐ **Storytelling:** Does the location meet the scene requirements and fit the director's tone?

☐ **Anachronism:** Does the setting fit the time period and story setting?

Notes:

SIGHT

○ interior   ○ exterior

| YES | NO | Indoor staging: Does the crew, cast and gear fit inside? |

| YES | NO | VFX Need: Would anything need to be removed or added in post? |

YES NO **Wide Shot test:** Wide frame acceptable?

YES NO **Wide Shot test:** Any problematicvisual elements in the frame?

| YES | NO | Indoor staging: Any special production design needs? |

YES NO **360 test:** Are there any problematic directions that should be avoided?

| YES | NO | Sunlight: Any sunlight consideration? |

YES NO **Commercial clearance:** Any properties that require commercial clearance?

○ morning   ○ noon   ○ afternoon   ○ evening   ○ night

Notes:

SOUND

YES NO **HVAC:** Can you turn off the heating, ventilation and air conditioning unit?

YES NO **Reverberation:** Can you record clean dialog?

YES NO **Refrigerators:** Can you turn off any noisy ? appliances or refrigerators?

YES NO **Reverberation:** Do you need to dampen echoes in the space?

Notes:

SURROUNDINGS

[YES] [NO] **Roads & Traffic:** Noise or continuity issues from vehicles or pedestrians?

[YES] [NO] **Schools:** Noise or other issues connected with students?

[YES] [NO] **Playgrounds:** Will noise affected the sound or will people be in the frame?

[YES] [NO] **Factories:** Any noise generated from the machines or any road issues?

[YES] [NO] **Gas station:** Any noise or traffic issues?

[YES] [NO] **Parking:** Is there sufficient parking for talent, crew, and production vehicles?

[YES] [NO] **Airports:** Noise or activity and traffic issues and concerns?

[YES] [NO] **Air traffic:** Any significant air traffic overhead and sound concerns?

[YES] [NO] **Subway:** Will subway noise fit to the scene? Will it affect sound recording?

[YES] [NO] **Subway:** Will subway noise fit to the scene? Will it affect sound recording?

[YES] [NO] **Train station:** Will train noise fit in the scene? Any train appear in the frame?

[YES] [NO] **Staging Talent:** Is there a quiet place dedicated for talent, extras, crew?

[YES] [NO] **Restrooms:** Is there a enough restrooms for all?

Notes:

WEATHER

[YES] [NO] **Temperature:** Is there temperature control?

[YES] [NO] **Rain / snow:** Will precipitation have a potential impact on the shoot?

[YES] [NO] **Indoor:** Will sound from precipitation have a potential impact on the shoot?

Notes:

POWER

[ ] How many accessible outlets?

[YES] [NO] **Access:** Does the electrical crew has access to the circuit breaker box?

[YES] [NO] **Hair and makeup:** Is there a dedicated space and breaker for Hair & Makeup?

FACILITIES

[ ] How many people on set to every available bathroom?

[YES] [NO] Access to **Water Shut Off** in case of emergency

[YES] [NO] Access to **Gas Shut Off** in case of emergency

Notes:

CONTRACTS

[YES] [NO] **Contract:** Has the location owner sign the contract/location release?

[YES] [NO] **Insurance:** Does the production insurance cover the location?

Dates needed: Total number of days: Total cost:

Contact person:

Phone: email:

LOCATION SCOUTING CHECKLIST

Project:

Director:

Producer:

Location scout:

Scene: Scene Number:

Location name:

Address:

STORY

☐ **Storytelling:** Does the location meet the scene requirements and fit the director's tone?

☐ **Anachronism:** Does the setting fit the time period and story setting?

Notes:

SIGHT

○ interior   ○ exterior

YES | NO **Indoor staging:** Does the crew, cast and gear fit inside?

YES | NO **VFX Need:** Would anything need to be removed or added in post?

YES | NO **Wide Shot test:** Wide frame acceptable?

YES | NO **Wide Shot test:** Any problematic visual elements in the frame?

YES | NO **360 test:** Are there any problematic directions that should be avoided?

YES | NO **Commercial clearance:** Any properties that require commercial clearance?

YES | NO **Indoor staging:** Any special production design needs?

YES | NO **Sunlight:** Any sunlight consideration?

○ morning   ○ noon   ○ afternoon   ○ evening   ○ night

Notes:

SOUND

YES | NO **HVAC:** Can you turn off the heating, ventilation and air conditioning unit?

YES | NO **Refrigerators:** Can you turn off any noisy? appliances or refrigerators?

YES | NO **Reverberation:** Can you record clean dialog?

YES | NO **Reverberation:** Do you need to dampen echoes in the space?

Notes:

LOCATION SCOUTING CHECKLIST

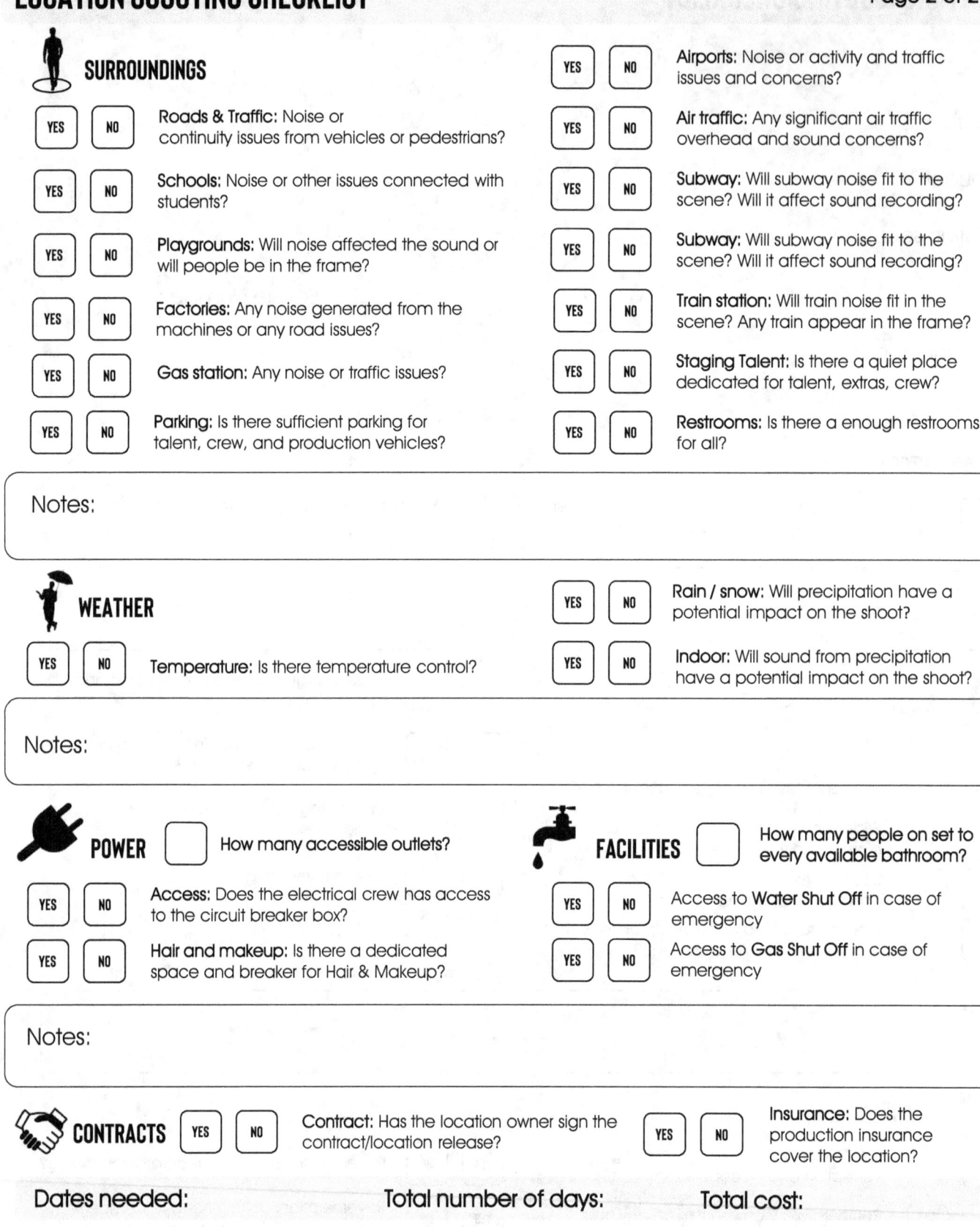

SURROUNDINGS

[YES] [NO] **Roads & Traffic:** Noise or continuity issues from vehicles or pedestrians?

[YES] [NO] **Schools:** Noise or other issues connected with students?

[YES] [NO] **Playgrounds:** Will noise affected the sound or will people be in the frame?

[YES] [NO] **Factories:** Any noise generated from the machines or any road issues?

[YES] [NO] **Gas station:** Any noise or traffic issues?

[YES] [NO] **Parking:** Is there sufficient parking for talent, crew, and production vehicles?

[YES] [NO] **Airports:** Noise or activity and traffic issues and concerns?

[YES] [NO] **Air traffic:** Any significant air traffic overhead and sound concerns?

[YES] [NO] **Subway:** Will subway noise fit to the scene? Will it affect sound recording?

[YES] [NO] **Subway:** Will subway noise fit to the scene? Will it affect sound recording?

[YES] [NO] **Train station:** Will train noise fit in the scene? Any train appear in the frame?

[YES] [NO] **Staging Talent:** Is there a quiet place dedicated for talent, extras, crew?

[YES] [NO] **Restrooms:** Is there a enough restrooms for all?

Notes:

WEATHER

[YES] [NO] **Temperature:** Is there temperature control?

[YES] [NO] **Rain / snow:** Will precipitation have a potential impact on the shoot?

[YES] [NO] **Indoor:** Will sound from precipitation have a potential impact on the shoot?

Notes:

POWER

[ ] How many accessible outlets?

[YES] [NO] **Access:** Does the electrical crew has access to the circuit breaker box?

[YES] [NO] **Hair and makeup:** Is there a dedicated space and breaker for Hair & Makeup?

FACILITIES

[ ] How many people on set to every available bathroom?

[YES] [NO] Access to **Water Shut Off** in case of emergency

[YES] [NO] Access to **Gas Shut Off** in case of emergency

Notes:

CONTRACTS

[YES] [NO] **Contract:** Has the location owner sign the contract/location release?

[YES] [NO] **Insurance:** Does the production insurance cover the location?

Dates needed: Total number of days: Total cost:

Contact person:

Phone: email:

LOCATION SCOUTING CHECKLIST

Project:

Director:

Producer:

Location scout:

Scene: Scene Number:

Location name:

Address:

STORY

☐ **Storytelling:** Does the location meet the scene requirements and fit the director's tone?

☐ **Anachronism:** Does the setting fit the time period and story setting?

Notes:

SIGHT

○ interior   ○ exterior

[YES] [NO] **Wide Shot test:** Wide frame acceptable?

[YES] [NO] **Wide Shot test:** Any problematicvisual elements in the frame?

[YES] [NO] **360 test:** Are there any problematic directions that should be avoided?

[YES] [NO] **Commercial clearance:** Any properties that require commercial clearance?

[YES] [NO] **Indoor staging:** Does the crew, cast and gear fit inside?

[YES] [NO] **VFX Need:** Would anything need to be removed or added in post?

[YES] [NO] **Indoor staging:** Any special production design needs?

[YES] [NO] **Sunlight:** Any sunlight consideration?

○ morning   ○ noon   ○ afternoon   ○ evening   ○ night

Notes:

SOUND

[YES] [NO] **HVAC:** Can you turn off the heating, ventilation and air conditioning unit?

[YES] [NO] **Refrigerators:** Can you turn off any noisy ? appliances or refrigerators?

[YES] [NO] **Reverberation:** Can you record clean dialog?

[YES] [NO] **Reverberation:** Do you need to dampen echoes in the space?

Notes:

SURROUNDINGS

YES **NO** — **Roads & Traffic:** Noise or continuity issues from vehicles or pedestrians?

YES **NO** — **Schools:** Noise or other issues connected with students?

YES **NO** — **Playgrounds:** Will noise affected the sound or will people be in the frame?

YES **NO** — **Factories:** Any noise generated from the machines or any road issues?

YES **NO** — **Gas station:** Any noise or traffic issues?

YES **NO** — **Parking:** Is there sufficient parking for talent, crew, and production vehicles?

YES **NO** — **Airports:** Noise or activity and traffic issues and concerns?

YES **NO** — **Air traffic:** Any significant air traffic overhead and sound concerns?

YES **NO** — **Subway:** Will subway noise fit to the scene? Will it affect sound recording?

YES **NO** — **Subway:** Will subway noise fit to the scene? Will it affect sound recording?

YES **NO** — **Train station:** Will train noise fit in the scene? Any train appear in the frame?

YES **NO** — **Staging Talent:** Is there a quiet place dedicated for talent, extras, crew?

YES **NO** — **Restrooms:** Is there a enough restrooms for all?

Notes:

WEATHER

YES **NO** — **Temperature:** Is there temperature control?

YES **NO** — **Rain / snow:** Will precipitation have a potential impact on the shoot?

YES **NO** — **Indoor:** Will sound from precipitation have a potential impact on the shoot?

Notes:

POWER

[ ] How many accessible outlets?

YES **NO** — **Access:** Does the electrical crew has access to the circuit breaker box?

YES **NO** — **Hair and makeup:** Is there a dedicated space and breaker for Hair & Makeup?

FACILITIES

[ ] How many people on set to every available bathroom?

YES **NO** — Access to **Water Shut Off** in case of emergency

YES **NO** — Access to **Gas Shut Off** in case of emergency

Notes:

CONTRACTS

YES **NO** — **Contract:** Has the location owner sign the contract/location release?

YES **NO** — **Insurance:** Does the production insurance cover the location?

Dates needed: Total number of days: Total cost:

Contact person:

Phone: email:

Project:

Director:

Producer:

Location scout:

Scene: Scene Number:

Location name:

Address:

STORY

☐ **Storytelling:** Does the location meet the scene requirements and fit the director's tone?

☐ **Anachronism:** Does the setting fit the time period and story setting?

Notes:

SIGHT

○ interior   ○ exterior

YES	NO	Indoor staging: Does the crew, cast and gear fit inside?
YES	NO	VFX Need: Would anything need to be removed or added in post?
YES	NO	Indoor staging: Any special production design needs?
YES	NO	Sunlight: Any sunlight consideration?

YES	NO	**Wide Shot test:** Wide frame acceptable?
YES	NO	**Wide Shot test:** Any problematic visual elements in the frame?
YES	NO	**360 test:** Are there any problematic directions that should be avoided?
YES	NO	**Commercial clearance:** Any properties that require commercial clearance?

○ morning   ○ noon   ○ afternoon   ○ evening   ○ night

Notes:

SOUND

| YES | NO | **HVAC:** Can you turn off the heating, ventilation and air conditioning unit? |
| YES | NO | **Refrigerators:** Can you turn off any noisy ? appliances or refrigerators? |

| YES | NO | **Reverberation:** Can you record clean dialog? |
| YES | NO | **Reverberation:** Do you need to dampen echoes in the space? |

Notes:

SURROUNDINGS

YES	NO	**Roads & Traffic:** Noise or continuity issues from vehicles or pedestrians?
YES	NO	**Schools:** Noise or other issues connected with students?
YES	NO	**Playgrounds:** Will noise affected the sound or will people be in the frame?
YES	NO	**Factories:** Any noise generated from the machines or any road issues?
YES	NO	**Gas station:** Any noise or traffic issues?
YES	NO	**Parking:** Is there sufficient parking for talent, crew, and production vehicles?

YES	NO	**Airports:** Noise or activity and traffic issues and concerns?
YES	NO	**Air traffic:** Any significant air traffic overhead and sound concerns?
YES	NO	**Subway:** Will subway noise fit to the scene? Will it affect sound recording?
YES	NO	**Subway:** Will subway noise fit to the scene? Will it affect sound recording?
YES	NO	**Train station:** Will train noise fit in the scene? Any train appear in the frame?
YES	NO	**Staging Talent:** Is there a quiet place dedicated for talent, extras, crew?
YES	NO	**Restrooms:** Is there a enough restrooms for all?

Notes:

WEATHER

| YES | NO | **Temperature:** Is there temperature control? |

| YES | NO | **Rain / snow:** Will precipitation have a potential impact on the shoot? |
| YES | NO | **Indoor:** Will sound from precipitation have a potential impact on the shoot? |

Notes:

POWER [ ] How many accessible outlets?

| YES | NO | **Access:** Does the electrical crew has access to the circuit breaker box? |
| YES | NO | **Hair and makeup:** Is there a dedicated space and breaker for Hair & Makeup? |

FACILITIES [ ] How many people on set to every available bathroom?

| YES | NO | Access to **Water Shut Off** in case of emergency |
| YES | NO | Access to **Gas Shut Off** in case of emergency |

Notes:

CONTRACTS YES NO **Contract:** Has the location owner sign the contract/location release?

YES NO **Insurance:** Does the production insurance cover the location?

Dates needed: Total number of days: Total cost:

Contact person:

Phone: email:

LOCATION SCOUTING CHECKLIST

Project:

Director:

Producer:

Location scout:

Scene: Scene Number:

Location name:

Address:

STORY

☐ **Storytelling:** Does the location meet the scene requirements and fit the director's tone?

☐ **Anachronism:** Does the setting fit the time period and story setting?

Notes:

SIGHT

◯ interior   ◯ exterior

[YES] [NO] **Wide Shot test:** Wide frame acceptable?

[YES] [NO] **Wide Shot test:** Any problematicvisual elements in the frame?

[YES] [NO] **360 test:** Are there any problematic directions that should be avoided?

[YES] [NO] **Commercial clearance:** Any properties that require commercial clearance?

[YES] [NO] **Indoor staging:** Does the crew, cast and gear fit inside?

[YES] [NO] **VFX Need:** Would anything need to be removed or added in post?

[YES] [NO] **Indoor staging:** Any special production design needs?

[YES] [NO] **Sunlight:** Any sunlight consideration?

◯ morning ◯ noon ◯ afternoon ◯ evening ◯ night

Notes:

SOUND

[YES] [NO] **HVAC:** Can you turn off the heating, ventilation and air conditioning unit?

[YES] [NO] **Refrigerators:** Can you turn off any noisy ? appliances or refrigerators?

[YES] [NO] **Reverberation:** Can you record clean dialog?

[YES] [NO] **Reverberation:** Do you need to dampen echoes in the space?

Notes:

SURROUNDINGS

YES	NO	
		Roads & Traffic: Noise or continuity issues from vehicles or pedestrians?
		Schools: Noise or other issues connected with students?
		Playgrounds: Will noise affected the sound or will people be in the frame?
		Factories: Any noise generated from the machines or any road issues?
		Gas station: Any noise or traffic issues?
		Parking: Is there sufficient parking for talent, crew, and production vehicles?

YES	NO	
		Airports: Noise or activity and traffic issues and concerns?
		Air traffic: Any significant air traffic overhead and sound concerns?
		Subway: Will subway noise fit to the scene? Will it affect sound recording?
		Subway: Will subway noise fit to the scene? Will it affect sound recording?
		Train station: Will train noise fit in the scene? Any train appear in the frame?
		Staging Talent: Is there a quiet place dedicated for talent, extras, crew?
		Restrooms: Is there a enough restrooms for all?

Notes:

WEATHER

YES	NO	
		Temperature: Is there temperature control?

YES	NO	
		Rain / snow: Will precipitation have a potential impact on the shoot?
		Indoor: Will sound from precipitation have a potential impact on the shoot?

Notes:

POWER

☐ How many accessible outlets?

YES	NO	
		Access: Does the electrical crew has access to the circuit breaker box?
		Hair and makeup: Is there a dedicated space and breaker for Hair & Makeup?

FACILITIES

☐ How many people on set to every available bathroom?

YES	NO	
		Access to **Water Shut Off** in case of emergency
		Access to **Gas Shut Off** in case of emergency

Notes:

CONTRACTS

YES	NO	
		Contract: Has the location owner sign the contract/location release?

YES	NO	
		Insurance: Does the production insurance cover the location?

Dates needed: Total number of days: Total cost:

Contact person:

Phone: email:

LOCATION SCOUTING CHECKLIST

Project:

Director:

Producer:

Location scout:

Scene: Scene Number:

Location name:

Address:

STORY

☐ **Storytelling:** Does the location meet the scene requirements and fit the director's tone?

☐ **Anachronism:** Does the setting fit the time period and story setting?

Notes:

SIGHT

◯ interior   ◯ exterior

[YES] [NO] **Wide Shot test:** Wide frame acceptable?

[YES] [NO] **Wide Shot test:** Any problematicvisual elements in the frame?

[YES] [NO] **360 test:** Are there any problematic directions that should be avoided?

[YES] [NO] **Commercial clearance:** Any properties that require commercial clearance?

[YES] [NO] **Indoor staging:** Does the crew, cast and gear fit inside?

[YES] [NO] **VFX Need:** Would anything need to be removed or added in post?

[YES] [NO] **Indoor staging:** Any special production design needs?

[YES] [NO] **Sunlight:** Any sunlight consideration?

◯ morning   ◯ noon   ◯ afternoon   ◯ evening   ◯ night

Notes:

SOUND

[YES] [NO] **HVAC:** Can you turn off the heating, ventilation and air conditioning unit?

[YES] [NO] **Refrigerators:** Can you turn off any noisy ? appliances or refrigerators?

[YES] [NO] **Reverberation:** Can you record clean dialog?

[YES] [NO] **Reverberation:** Do you need to dampen echoes in the space?

Notes:

SURROUNDINGS

YES **NO** — **Roads & Traffic:** Noise or continuity issues from vehicles or pedestrians?

YES **NO** — **Schools:** Noise or other issues connected with students?

YES **NO** — **Playgrounds:** Will noise affected the sound or will people be in the frame?

YES **NO** — **Factories:** Any noise generated from the machines or any road issues?

YES **NO** — **Gas station:** Any noise or traffic issues?

YES **NO** — **Parking:** Is there sufficient parking for talent, crew, and production vehicles?

YES **NO** — **Airports:** Noise or activity and traffic issues and concerns?

YES **NO** — **Air traffic:** Any significant air traffic overhead and sound concerns?

YES **NO** — **Subway:** Will subway noise fit to the scene? Will it affect sound recording?

YES **NO** — **Subway:** Will subway noise fit to the scene? Will it affect sound recording?

YES **NO** — **Train station:** Will train noise fit in the scene? Any train appear in the frame?

YES **NO** — **Staging Talent:** Is there a quiet place dedicated for talent, extras, crew?

YES **NO** — **Restrooms:** Is there a enough restrooms for all?

Notes:

WEATHER

YES **NO** — **Temperature:** Is there temperature control?

YES **NO** — **Rain / snow:** Will precipitation have a potential impact on the shoot?

YES **NO** — **Indoor:** Will sound from precipitation have a potential impact on the shoot?

Notes:

POWER

[ ] How many accessible outlets?

YES **NO** — **Access:** Does the electrical crew has access to the circuit breaker box?

YES **NO** — **Hair and makeup:** Is there a dedicated space and breaker for Hair & Makeup?

FACILITIES

[ ] How many people on set to every available bathroom?

YES **NO** — Access to **Water Shut Off** in case of emergency

YES **NO** — Access to **Gas Shut Off** in case of emergency

Notes:

CONTRACTS

YES **NO** — **Contract:** Has the location owner sign the contract/location release?

YES **NO** — **Insurance:** Does the production insurance cover the location?

Dates needed: Total number of days: Total cost:

Contact person:

Phone: email:

LOCATION SCOUTING CHECKLIST

Project:

Director:

Producer:

Location scout:

Scene: Scene Number:

Location name:

Address:

STORY

☐ **Storytelling:** Does the location meet the scene requirements and fit the director's tone?

☐ **Anachronism:** Does the setting fit the time period and story setting?

Notes:

SIGHT

○ interior   ○ exterior

[YES] [NO] **Wide Shot test:** Wide frame acceptable?

[YES] [NO] **Wide Shot test:** Any problematicvisual elements in the frame?

[YES] [NO] **360 test:** Are there any problematic directions that should be avoided?

[YES] [NO] **Commercial clearance:** Any properties that require commercial clearance?

[YES] [NO] **Indoor staging:** Does the crew, cast and gear fit inside?

[YES] [NO] **VFX Need:** Would anything need to be removed or added in post?

[YES] [NO] **Indoor staging:** Any special production design needs?

[YES] [NO] **Sunlight:** Any sunlight consideration?

○ morning ○ noon ○ afternoon ○ evening ○ night

Notes:

SOUND

[YES] [NO] **HVAC:** Can you turn off the heating, ventilation and air conditioning unit?

[YES] [NO] **Refrigerators:** Can you turn off any noisy ? appliances or refrigerators?

[YES] [NO] **Reverberation:** Can you record clean dialog?

[YES] [NO] **Reverberation:** Do you need to dampen echoes in the space?

Notes:

SURROUNDINGS

[YES] [NO] **Roads & Traffic:** Noise or continuity issues from vehicles or pedestrians?

[YES] [NO] **Schools:** Noise or other issues connected with students?

[YES] [NO] **Playgrounds:** Will noise affected the sound or will people be in the frame?

[YES] [NO] **Factories:** Any noise generated from the machines or any road issues?

[YES] [NO] **Gas station:** Any noise or traffic issues?

[YES] [NO] **Parking:** Is there sufficient parking for talent, crew, and production vehicles?

[YES] [NO] **Airports:** Noise or activity and traffic issues and concerns?

[YES] [NO] **Air traffic:** Any significant air traffic overhead and sound concerns?

[YES] [NO] **Subway:** Will subway noise fit to the scene? Will it affect sound recording?

[YES] [NO] **Subway:** Will subway noise fit to the scene? Will it affect sound recording?

[YES] [NO] **Train station:** Will train noise fit in the scene? Any train appear in the frame?

[YES] [NO] **Staging Talent:** Is there a quiet place dedicated for talent, extras, crew?

[YES] [NO] **Restrooms:** Is there a enough restrooms for all?

Notes:

WEATHER

[YES] [NO] **Temperature:** Is there temperature control?

[YES] [NO] **Rain / snow:** Will precipitation have a potential impact on the shoot?

[YES] [NO] **Indoor:** Will sound from precipitation have a potential impact on the shoot?

Notes:

POWER

[   ] How many accessible outlets?

[YES] [NO] **Access:** Does the electrical crew has access to the circuit breaker box?

[YES] [NO] **Hair and makeup:** Is there a dedicated space and breaker for Hair & Makeup?

FACILITIES

[   ] How many people on set to every available bathroom?

[YES] [NO] Access to **Water Shut Off** in case of emergency

[YES] [NO] Access to **Gas Shut Off** in case of emergency

Notes:

CONTRACTS

[YES] [NO] **Contract:** Has the location owner sign the contract/location release?

[YES] [NO] **Insurance:** Does the production insurance cover the location?

Dates needed: _____   Total number of days: _____   Total cost: _____

Contact person: _____

Phone: _____   email: _____

LOCATION SCOUTING CHECKLIST

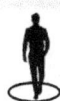 **SURROUNDINGS**

YES NO **Roads & Traffic:** Noise or continuity issues from vehicles or pedestrians?

YES NO **Schools:** Noise or other issues connected with students?

YES NO **Playgrounds:** Will noise affected the sound or will people be in the frame?

YES NO **Factories:** Any noise generated from the machines or any road issues?

YES NO **Gas station:** Any noise or traffic issues?

YES NO **Parking:** Is there sufficient parking for talent, crew, and production vehicles?

YES NO **Airports:** Noise or activity and traffic issues and concerns?

YES NO **Air traffic:** Any significant air traffic overhead and sound concerns?

YES NO **Subway:** Will subway noise fit to the scene? Will it affect sound recording?

YES NO **Subway:** Will subway noise fit to the scene? Will it affect sound recording?

YES NO **Train station:** Will train noise fit in the scene? Any train appear in the frame?

YES NO **Staging Talent:** Is there a quiet place dedicated for talent, extras, crew?

YES NO **Restrooms:** Is there a enough restrooms for all?

Notes:

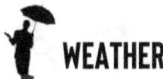 **WEATHER**

YES NO **Temperature:** Is there temperature control?

YES NO **Rain / snow:** Will precipitation have a potential impact on the shoot?

YES NO **Indoor:** Will sound from precipitation have a potential impact on the shoot?

Notes:

 POWER [ ] How many accessible outlets?

YES NO **Access:** Does the electrical crew has access to the circuit breaker box?

YES NO **Hair and makeup:** Is there a dedicated space and breaker for Hair & Makeup?

 FACILITIES [ ] How many people on set to every available bathroom?

YES NO Access to **Water Shut Off** in case of emergency

YES NO Access to **Gas Shut Off** in case of emergency

Notes:

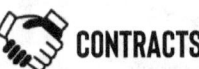 **CONTRACTS** YES NO **Contract:** Has the location owner sign the contract/location release?

 YES NO **Insurance:** Does the production insurance cover the location?

Dates needed: Total number of days: Total cost:

Contact person:

Phone: email:

LOCATION SCOUTING CHECKLIST

SURROUNDINGS

YES NO **Roads & Traffic:** Noise or continuity issues from vehicles or pedestrians?

YES NO **Schools:** Noise or other issues connected with students?

YES NO **Playgrounds:** Will noise affected the sound or will people be in the frame?

YES NO **Factories:** Any noise generated from the machines or any road issues?

YES NO **Gas station:** Any noise or traffic issues?

YES NO **Parking:** Is there sufficient parking for talent, crew, and production vehicles?

YES NO **Airports:** Noise or activity and traffic issues and concerns?

YES NO **Air traffic:** Any significant air traffic overhead and sound concerns?

YES NO **Subway:** Will subway noise fit to the scene? Will it affect sound recording?

YES NO **Subway:** Will subway noise fit to the scene? Will it affect sound recording?

YES NO **Train station:** Will train noise fit in the scene? Any train appear in the frame?

YES NO **Staging Talent:** Is there a quiet place dedicated for talent, extras, crew?

YES NO **Restrooms:** Is there a enough restrooms for all?

Notes:

WEATHER

YES NO **Temperature:** Is there temperature control?

YES NO **Rain / snow:** Will precipitation have a potential impact on the shoot?

YES NO **Indoor:** Will sound from precipitation have a potential impact on the shoot?

Notes:

POWER

[ ] How many accessible outlets?

YES NO **Access:** Does the electrical crew has access to the circuit breaker box?

YES NO **Hair and makeup:** Is there a dedicated space and breaker for Hair & Makeup?

FACILITIES

[ ] How many people on set to every available bathroom?

YES NO Access to **Water Shut Off** in case of emergency

YES NO Access to **Gas Shut Off** in case of emergency

Notes:

CONTRACTS

YES NO **Contract:** Has the location owner sign the contract/location release?

YES NO **Insurance:** Does the production insurance cover the location?

Dates needed: Total number of days: Total cost:

Contact person:

Phone: email: